IT HAPPENED IN
UTAH

SECOND EDITION

Gayen and Tom Wharton

TWODOT®

GUILFORD, CONNECTICUT
HELENA, MONTANA
AN IMPRINT OF THE GLOBE PEQUOT PRESS

A · **T W O D O T**® · **B O O K**

Copyright © 2007 Morris Book Publishing, LLC

The previous edition of this book was published by Falcon Publishing, Inc. in 1998.

Text design by Nancy Freeborn
Map by M. A. Dubé © 2007 Morris Book Publishing, LLC
Front cover photo: Joining of the Central Pacific and Union Pacific Lines at Promontory Point, Utah, May 10, 1869. Library of Congress, LC-USZ62-57524
Back cover photo: Mormon Temple grounds, ca. 1912. Library of Congress, LC-USZ62-135252

Library of Congress Cataloging-in-Publication Data
Wharton, Gayen, 1950-
  It happened in Utah/Gayen and Tom Wharton.—2nd ed.
    p. cm.—(It happened in series)
  Includes bibliographical references and index.
  ISBN-13: 978-0-7627-4482-4
  ISBN-10: 0-7627-4482-0
  1. Utah—History—Anecdotes. 2. Utah—Biography—Anecdotes. I. Wharton, Tom, 1950- II. Title.
  F826.6.W47 2007
  979.2—dc22

                                                            2006038774

Manufactured in the United States of America
Second Edition/First Printing

THIS BOOK HAS BEEN IN:
1- FREEPORT, FL, U.S.A.
2.

Our thanks to our grandparents who told us stories
and shared their history.

CONTENTS

CONTENTS

ACKNOWLEDGMENTS

Special thanks to those individuals who helped with our research: Mel Bashore from the LDS Church Library and the staff at Utah State Historic Society were invaluable. Many thanks to June Omura Aoki, Roy Webb, Marion Dunn, Alexis Kelner, Patrick Hearty, Betty Stanton, Madge Tomsic, Lori Perez, Kathy Hart, Dee Holliday, Rich Ingebretson, Ken Sleight, Dick Wilson, Edward Thomas, and Bob Woody. The *Salt Lake Tribune* also helped provide valuable research materials.

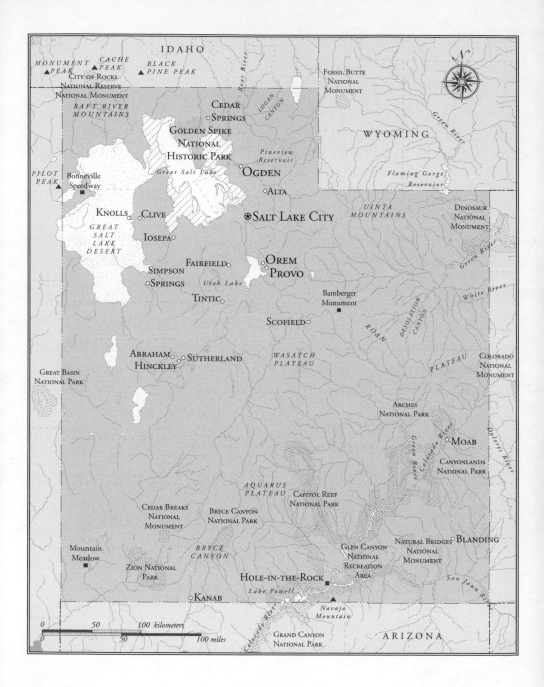

IDAHO

▲ MONUMENT PEAK   ▲ CACHE PEAK   BLACK ▲ PINE PEAK

CITY OF ROCKS NATIONAL RESERVE NATIONAL MONUMENT

FOSSIL BUTTE NATIONAL MONUMENT

RAFT RIVER MOUNTAINS

CEDAR SPRINGS

GOLDEN SPIKE NATIONAL HISTORIC PARK

Bear River

LOGAN CANYON

WYOMING

Green River

Pineview Reservoir

Great Salt Lake

OGDEN

Flaming Gorge Reservoir

PILOT PEAK ▲

Bonneville Speedway

ALTA

✸SALT LAKE CITY

UINTA MOUNTAINS

DINOSAUR NATIONAL MONUMENT

KNOLLS   CLIVE

GREAT SALT LAKE DESERT

IOSEPA

Green River

FAIRFIELD   OREM PROVO

SIMPSON SPRINGS   *Utah Lake*

TINTIC

Bamberger Monument

White River

GREAT BASIN NATIONAL PARK

SCOFIELD

ROAN

DESOLATION CANYON

PLATEAU

COLORADO NATIONAL MONUMENT

ABRAHAM   SUTHERLAND HINCKLEY

WASATCH PLATEAU

ARCHES NATIONAL PARK

Green River

Colorado River

MOAB

Dolores River

CANYONLANDS NATIONAL PARK

AQUARUS PLATEAU

CEDAR BREAKS NATIONAL MONUMENT

BRYCE CANYON NATIONAL PARK

CAPITOL REEF NATIONAL PARK

NATURAL BRIDGES NATIONAL MONUMENT

BLANDING

Mountain Meadow

BRYCE CANYON

GLEN CANYON NATIONAL RECREATION AREA

ZION NATIONAL PARK

HOLE-IN-THE-ROCK

Lake Powell

San Juan River

KANAB

Navajo Mountain ▲

Colorado River

GRAND CANYON NATIONAL PARK

ARIZONA

0   50   100 *kilometers*

0   50   100 *miles*

UTAH

PREFACE

We chose the stories for *It Happened in Utah* because they grabbed us—and drew us into reading more about the history of our remarkable state. *It Happened in Utah* is meant to be a different kind of history book. Utah's unique history and culture—from the arrival of the mountain men in 1825 to the Winter Olympic Games in 2002—are chronicled here in an unusual way. Each chapter tells the story of a single, brief event that helped shape Utah. Each provides a look at one aspect of the history of the state.

Utah's history was strongly influenced by the Mormon settlement of the area. The stories here portray this dynamic and colorful people and tell of their interactions with non-Mormons within and outside the state. We have tried to capture more of Utah's rich cultural, ethnic, and gender diversity by recounting both major events—the completion of the transcontinental railroad, for example—and smaller, unusual occurrences, such as the election of an all-female town council in Kanab in 1912.

It Happened in Utah chronicles the triumphs and failures in Utah's history. "Mountain Meadow Massacre" recalls a tragedy. "Ab Jenkins Is Fast on the Salt Flats" tells the story of an amazing success that only could have happened in Utah.

We hope that students of history of all ages, and anyone who loves a good story, will enjoy *It Happened in Utah*.

A FUR TRADERS' FIGHT

- 1825 -

BY THE TIME PETER SKENE OGDEN'S GROUP REACHED THE Great Salt Lake in May of 1825, they had struggled through deep snowdrifts and achieved a hazardous mountain crossing. War parties of Bloods and Blackfeet had attacked, costing them the lives of both horses and men.

Around the same time, Etienne Provost entered the Great Salt Lake area. A French-Canadian fur trader, Provost led a motley group of Canadian, Spanish, and even Russian mountain men out of Taos, New Mexico. Provost had run into trouble with the Spanish government in New Mexico over his trapping activities and had spent time in Santa Fe dungeons. Now he looked to provide beaver pelts for Spanish Trail traders.

On this May 1825 trip to the Great Salt Lake, Provost ventured farther north. He soon found himself in the same territory with the British group under Peter Skene Ogden. To crowd matters further, John Weber showed up with an American party trapping for fur traders William H. Ashley and Andrew Henry. With all these men in the same area after the same limited resource, trouble was inevitable.

Before they encountered Ogden, Provost's party met up with Weber and the Americans. The Canadian and his men listened to the talk of Jedediah Smith, an American trapper working for William H. Ashley. Smith had been in Oregon Territory on business. He had left there at the same time as Ogden. During the trip south, he had kept an eye on Ogden's party. As soon as Smith heard Weber was in the area, he set off to find the American leader with a report that could not be ignored: Ogden was flying the Union Jack and talking as if this country belonged to Britain.

Johnson Gardner, a member of Provost's group, grew angry as he listened. Before joining Provost, Gardner had trapped the Missouri River with William Ashley and had traversed South Pass with Weber. An independent mountain man, Gardner considered himself a loyal American. The trapper led both parties to a vote to show Ogden he was not in British territory; they would pay the British a visit in the morning.

On May 23, 1825, Johnson Gardner and twenty-five others rode past Ogden's camp, brazenly flying their American flag. For unknown reasons, Weber and Provost did not accompany their men. That night, while both parties camped nearby, Gardner spoke with Ogden and his clerk, William Kittson. In no uncertain terms, he informed them that they were trespassing on American territory and must leave immediately. Gardner offered to pay $3.50 a pound for their beaver pelts, which was much more than they would get from Hudson's Bay Company. Most damaging of all, Gardner accused the company of treating its men like slaves. He offered to help any mountain man in Ogden's company who wanted to desert and join Provost's group.

Such an offer got Ogden's men thinking. Many Hudson's Bay Company trappers were Iroquois and Canadian freemen. They recognized the truth in Gardner's words. They paid high prices to the company for supplies and received low prices for their furs. They were always in debt to the company. After heated words and minor fighting, a small group of trappers from Ogden's company left with Gardner.

But Gardner wasn't finished. He returned to the British camp the next morning and demanded that Ogden tell everyone in which country they were camped. Ogden replied that no one was sure who owned the valley. It belongs to the United States and the British must leave, Gardner thundered back. (What Ogden—and perhaps even Gardner—didn't know was that they were actually in Mexican territory according to the Adams Onis Treaty of 1819.) Ogden insisted he would not leave until his government told him to do so. If Ogden didn't leave, Gardner threatened, the British trappers would be in danger.

Gardner left Ogden's tent and went to the lodge of John Grey, a part-Indian, part-white leader of the Iroquois who were trapping for Ogden. Grey agreed that his people had been treated poorly by the British. The only reason they had not deserted sooner, he told Gardner, was because they had not met the Americans. On Grey's order, the Iroquois dismantled their lodges. Ogden saw his supplies disappearing as well. While Gardner and his men pointed guns at Ogden, he ran here and there, trying to recover as much property as he could. He managed to salvage goods from men who were not in camp that day, including three thousand beaver skins. His clerk, Kittson, hurried to save the horses they had lent the Iroquois.

The Americans fired no shots, but they hurled plenty of insults and obscenities at the outnumbered British. Ogden and his remaining men could only watch as twenty-one more deserters took piles of beaver pelts over to the American camp.

Gardner and his men made camp for the night about half a mile away. At the British camp, Ogden doubled the watch, fearing the deserters would return to kill his men and steal everything. He decided to leave for safer territory the next morning.

As the British broke camp, Gardner and company showed up again and took two more of Ogden's men with them. Gardner rode off bragging that he would see Ogden at the Columbia River and at other northern posts the British thought they owned.

More men deserted Ogden as he headed north. However demoralized he was by his losses, he knew the deserters had a point. American fur companies paid trappers eight times what the British paid for beaver pelts. Ogden returned and made his report to Hudson's Bay Company, and the company changed the way it treated fur trappers, thus avoiding further revolts.

By 1850, most of the beaver were gone; the mountain men disappeared with them. One of the most colorful events in trapping history took place at what is now Ogden's Hole, a pretty mountain valley above the city of Ogden.

MOUNTAIN MAN JEDEDIAH SMITH
MEETS HIS MATCH

- 1827 -

JEDEDIAH SMITH THOUGHT HIS TROUBLES WERE OVER. He and his fur trader companions were about to embark on the last leg of their exploration of the Southwest. In a few days they would reach the annual fur trading rendezvous in the Rocky Mountains.

It seemed like a long time had passed since Smith and his partners, David E. Jackson and William L. Sublette, had bought General William Ashley's fur trading company. Then, just a year before—in the summer of 1826—Smith decided to take a party of men and explore the area between what has since become Utah and California. His excitement about seeing this new territory and the hope of finding many new sources of beaver made him optimistic.

Now, at the end of the expedition, he reconsidered the merits of his actions. The large group of men, horses, and mules he started with had dwindled to two men besides himself, seven horses, and two mules. Now, however, he had only to cross the Great Basin to reach home.

The land between Utah and California is made up of a series of valleys and mountain ranges. A basin or valley separates each mountain range from the next. Around the Great Salt Lake, streams that would normally run off into the sea end up in the lake or the surrounding mud flats. Having collected salt-bearing runoff for hundreds of thousands of years, the many water sources in the Great Basin are brackish.

On June 22, Smith and his remaining companions, Robert Evans and Silas Gobel, spent the night on the briny edge of a small salty lake. Here the Great Basin played its first prank. One of Smith's horses, trotting across some crusty mud, sank suddenly into the ooze up to its stomach. Try as they could, the men could not free the animal. A frustrated Smith killed the horse and salvaged what meat he could.

Smith and his friends decided to travel in the valleys and rocky foothills. Each mountain range they passed looked the same—snow-capped peaks with intermittent streams along their flanks. On June 23, the men shot at an antelope and missed. Luckily, they bagged two rabbits for dinner. They were getting tired of horse meat.

The next day, the men stopped twice for water. After that, the only water they found was too salty to drink. The party camped that night without water.

Smith got up early the next morning. He rode to the top of a nearby hill to scout what lay ahead. The desert seemed to stretch on forever. Then, on the way back, Smith's horse gave out on him. When he finally got back to camp, he evasively told Gobel and Evans that he had seen a dark spot on the horizon that must be water. He knew the truth would demoralize them.

Under a scorching sun, the men plodded on through the soft sand. Each step was an effort; each breath of dry air brought pangs of thirst. By late afternoon, the men could go no farther. Smith, who knew from his previous treks what had to be done, made Evans and Gobel join him in digging holes in the shade of a juniper tree. They buried themselves in the sand to cool off and rest. When the sun went down, they dug out and traveled on. Soon the men saw turtle-doves; according to Smith, this meant water was somewhere nearby. They searched for it in vain.

At ten that night, the men tried to sleep. Cruelly, their thirst brought on dreams of water. In the state he was in, Smith later wrote, gold and honors meant nothing to him. All he wanted was the clear, refreshing streams of the mountains.

At midmorning on June 25, Evans fell motionless under a juniper tree. He refused to get up. Smith and Gobel, promising to return for him, continued in search of water. Some time later, they saw Indians headed for the place where they had left Evans. They heard gunshots and saw smoke. They didn't turn around. Doggedly, they trudged on.

Three miles later, they came upon a spring. Gobel jumped right into the water. Smith poured water over his head and down his throat as fast as he could. The two men filled their water horns and hurried back to the juniper tree.

Evans was still there. He hadn't even seen the Indians; he had fired shots and lit a fire to make sure his companions could find him again. Smith poured a mixture of water and horse meat from a large kettle into Evans's mouth. When Evans felt strong enough, the trio returned to the spring to drink their fill and recuperate.

How curious it was, Smith reflected in his journal, that a hungry man takes several days to recover, but a thirsty man seems to revive much sooner. "Hunger can be endured twice as long as thirst." During the day they spent at the freshwater spring, the three saw several Indians on the hilltops looking down at them. The white men sat still and looked back, no doubt wondering (among other things) how these people could survive in such a harsh environment. The Paiute and Goshute who lived in the Great Basin seemed primitive to men like Smith. He claimed they survived on insects, lizards, small game, and plants, thus he saw them as inferior to other tribes he encountered. Ironically, the Paiutes and Goshutes knew much more about the Great Basin than Smith, most importantly where to find fresh water. But the Indians on the hilltop did not come any closer to protest.

On the morning of June 26, Smith, Evans, and Gobel trudged on to the north, passing several more brackish springs. They encountered a group of Shoshone Indians. Smith recognized the nomads and was able to communicate with them. A few days' ride to the northeast, they told him, he and his men would find plenty of buffalo. Smith pressed them for information about the Great Salt Lake, the landmark that would show him the way home to the Cache Valley and the rendezvous. The Shoshone seemed to know nothing about it.

But on June 27, the three men found cause to celebrate. They saw the Great Salt Lake ahead, large and blue and ringed to the east by the prodigious Wasatch Mountains. Safe at last! To Smith, the Great Salt Lake offered a homecoming. He loved the place. The walk around the southern end of the lake seemed easy. Even crossing the Jordan River at flood stage felt like a happy adventure.

A few days later, the three fur trappers made it to the mountain man rendezvous at Bear Lake. They were down to one horse and one mule. Their friends had feared them lost. In jubilation, the men at the rendezvous fired a cannon. Smith, a man who was known for his disdain of alcohol, tobacco, and loose women, made no record in his journal of how he celebrated.

MORMON PIONEERS REACH ZION

- 1847 -

ORSON PRATT AND ERASTUS SNOW SCRAMBLED EAGERLY through groves of scrub oak. The men had gone ahead of their Mormon wagon train to scout a route. After three months and 1,300 miles of hard travel, the Mormons were about to reach their destination. It was late July and all were anxious to start farming before winter.

The Mormons had fled Nauvoo, Illinois, in 1846 after the murder of their prophet, Joseph Smith, in 1844. Smith had always hoped to move his people to a place where they would be left in peace, free from religious persecution. His successor, Brigham Young, was determined to carry out Smith's vision. Gleaning information from the experiences of explorer John C. Frémont, California entrepreneur Lansford Hastings, and various mountain men, Young chose a safe haven—the valley of the Great Salt Lake.

After they were forced from their homes in Nauvoo, the Mormons spent a difficult winter in Winter Quarters, Nebraska. In April of 1847, Young led an advance Mormon wagon train across the river. The party consisted of 143 men, including Pratt and Snow, three women, two children, and seventy-two wagons. Young planned to blaze a trail for the approximately 14,000 church members who would follow.

Using horses and mules to pull his wagons, Young hoped to make good time. Later companies would use slower, stronger oxen. Once the advance party of Mormons reached the valley, they would return along the route to clear rocks and brush, making the way more passable for the thousands of wagons to come.

At Fort Laramie, a second group of seventeen Mormons from Mississippi, including six women, and a handful of Mormon Battalion members joined Young's party. Several of the Battalion members (Mormon men who had volunteered to serve the United States government) had fallen ill. Unable to follow the Battalion on its trek to California, these men had spent the winter in Pueblo, Colorado, before joining Young's party. Together, the Mormons continued the grueling journey westward.

After the wagon train crossed the Continental Divide, a new kind of hardship befell its members: a disease they called mountain fever. The horrible aches, chills, and fever that spread from wagon to wagon made travel exceedingly painful. Brigham Young was among the ailing pioneers. He divided the advance company into thirds. A group led by Orson Pratt was sent ahead. The largest number of wagons would follow more slowly. Young and eight to ten wagons came last, taking time to recuperate.

The day Pratt and Snow went scouting, their group and the main group had rejoined. The scouts were following the remnants of a trail the Donner-Reed emigrant party had forged the year before.

At one point, the two found their path ascending a steep hill. Balking at the hill, Snow wondered why the Donner party had not just followed the creek bed downhill. He decided to look for an easier route. Thick underbrush lined the rocky creek. Soon, Snow was crawling through the bushes, looking for an opening. He heard a warning rattle and carefully retreated from what he knew must be a dangerous rattlesnake. Snow and Pratt reconsidered. They returned to the hill for a second look. It was like many others the company had climbed, but steeper. They clambered on up.

At the summit of what is now Donner Hill, the two men whooped for joy. There, spread out before them, at the foot of tall, forested mountains, was the valley of the Great Salt Lake. The lake's blue waters shimmered to the far west. From mountain canyons, shrub- and tree-lined streams flowed into the valley. The air was fresh and clear.

The two men couldn't resist. They hurried down the trail from the bench into the valley, taking mental notes about their new home as they went. They found a good site for a first settlement and returned to the rest of the two parties with the great news.

The next day, July 21, was a long one. Pratt's group and the main group suffered through it together. As they rested that night near the brushy creek bed (now known as Emigration Creek), they calculated they had gone 14 miles in thirteen hours. They were exhausted. Despite his encounter with the rattler, Pratt decided to blaze a trail down Emigration Creek instead of up Donner Hill.

It is interesting to imagine Salt Lake City as it was then. The wagons probably came down along the creek until they reached a bench near present-day This Is the Place State Park. From here, they turned south, paralleling the stretch that is now Wasatch Boulevard, then traveled west. They set up their first camp near Fifth East Street and Seventeenth South Street. During the sesquicentennial celebration in 1997, the site was dedicated as Encampment Park.

Parley's Creek flowed past the Mormons' campsite, and the stock had plenty of tall grass to feast upon. On July 23, the group moved to the spot Snow and Pratt had chosen at the mouth of what is now called City Creek Canyon, traveling northwest past present-day Liberty Park. By noon, the men were plowing the hard but rich earth and planting potatoes and corn. They diverted the creek to irrigate the crops; the pioneers knew they could not depend on rainfall in this part of the world. In a small grove of cottonwood trees and willows, they set up their tents.

Pratt sent two of the settlers, John Pack and Joseph Matthews, to report their progress to Brigham Young. The last section of the advance group had not yet entered the valley. The two men rode back to Young's group, stopping to stabilize two bridges along the way.

Still weak with fever, Young lay in the back of Wilford Woodruff's carriage. Woodruff's journal entry on the day they set eyes on the beautiful fertile valley reflects Young's satisfaction and Woodruff's wonder and admiration.

Young's own feelings and words at seeing the Great Salt Lake valley are lost. Later, Woodruff said that Young exclaimed, "This is the right place!" But Young and others later declared they had entered a desert. Harriet Young, Brigham's wife, was apparently so disappointed she didn't want to stay. The valley could not have compared with the forested woodlands the Mormons had left back east. But Young had plans. He wanted to plant trees and crops and make the valley blossom. Doubters were treated to a sound rebuke that afternoon in the form of a heavy rainstorm.

The group rested the next day, Sunday, and on Monday, work began again. The irrigation water had softened the ground for plowing. The pioneers planted corn, oats, turnips, buckwheat, cabbage, potatoes, and peach and apple trees.

By Wednesday, Young had chosen a site for the first Mormon temple at the fork of what is now City Creek. Thus the Mormons began building their promised land. Converts from all over the world would come to this valley.

On Thursday, another group of Mississippi Mormons and Mormon Battalion members entered the Great Salt Lake valley. Rejoining the companions that had met the Mormon wagon train at Fort Laramie, they raised the settlement's population to 450.

Young carried out his plan for the city of Salt Lake. He directed the laying out of 135 ten-acre blocks. The settlers built streets wide enough for a wagon team to turn around in; today, the same streets accommodate four lanes of traffic. Three public squares were established for recreation and contemplation.

Young constructed Old Fort around his settlement. Adobe walls surrounded the original twenty-nine log cabins. Aware that the Ute Indians claimed the more fertile Utah Valley to the south, Young had declined to settle there. He would work patiently with the original inhabitants of the territory to build his empire.

The advance company had done their job well, establishing a sound route for the rest of the Mormon pioneers to follow. Gold seekers would join immigrants on the Mormons' trail. Those who came later would find a city, roughly laid out, irrigated fields, and crops already growing. The pioneers in the advance company and those who came later that summer were grateful for the fresh food because no one had been able to bring enough supplies to last the winter.

After a summer of backbreaking work, almost half the men in the Great Salt Lake valley left again. They would return to Winter Quarters to guide more Mormons to Salt Lake City where they would help establish a home for Mormons in the West.

MOUNTAIN MEADOW MASSACRE

- 1857 -

IN A MOUNTAIN MEADOW NORTH OF ST. GEORGE, one can hear the grass murmur. If only it could talk, it might explain what happened here on September 11, 1857, when more than 120 people died. Some of their bones were buried beneath the soil. Others were carried off by animals. Today, a monument stands in the meadow, engraved with words that attempt to explain what happened. The words, however, seem inadequate because after all these years, no one knows the truth.

The story of the Mountain Meadow Massacre is both a mystery and a tragedy. Those who perpetrated the slaughter either gave conflicting reports of events or kept a vow of silence. The motives for killing a wagon train of hopeful immigrants can only be guessed at. Who could have such malice, hate, or vengeance in their hearts?

The story begins in the summer of 1857. A wagon train led by Alexander Fancher and George Baker left Arkansas for California. Fancher had been to the West Coast earlier, scouting for land to purchase. The two men brought forty extra teams of horses and mules, eight hundred head of cattle, and even a valuable stallion for start-ing a new ranch. By all accounts, the train was well equipped. Fam-ilies rode in wagons, hacks, buggies, and carriages. Only Baker's mother had refused to go. A premonition told her disaster would strike in the West.

All went according to plan until the wagon train reached Salt Lake City later that summer. There, the emigrants learned that Pres-ident James Buchanan had bowed to political pressure and sent an army led by Colonel Albert Sidney Johnston west to "take care of" the Mormons.

No one knew what such orders meant. Some thought Johnston might take over the Mormons' government. The Mormons feared violence—a repeat of their experience in Nauvoo, Illinois, eleven years before, and Jackson County, Missouri, before that. Their prophet, Joseph Smith, had been murdered in Carthage, Illinois, in 1844. Mobs had looted and burned Mormon homes, forcing the Mormons to flee Nauvoo. From there, they headed west to find peace. Now, expecting the arrival of Colonel Johnston and his invad-ing forces, Mormon men organized into militias and drilled vigor-ously all over the territory.

Instead of being welcomed to the Salt Lake Valley as previous wagon trains had been, the Fancher party met with suspicion and distrust—some thought they might be spies. Though the Mormons usually traded goods for money with emigrants, they refused to have anything to do with these visitors from the East. Mormon leader Brigham Young told his followers not to trade with any Gentile (non-Mormon); they must save all they had in preparation for the trial to come. The wagon train received a similar reception in every Utah town along the route.

Members of the wagon company reacted with belligerence. They told the Mormons they, too, came from Missouri and were glad the

Mormon prophet Joseph Smith had been killed. They taunted the Mormons, saying they would repay their rudeness later by returning to wipe out the settlers. The Fancher party traveled south. Reports circulated that they had poisoned the water supply outside of Fillmore. In Cedar City, members of the wagon train cursed the Mormons in public while brazenly attempting to help themselves to food supplies.

As emigrants traveling through Utah in those days, the Fancher party had other enemies as well. The pioneers had problems with bands of Ute and Paiute Indians in the past. This time, Brigham Young appeared more than willing to exploit this friction. The Mormons worked hard to stay on good terms with the Indians. They fed them on occasion and provided for them as much as they could. Some Indians had even joined the Mormon Church. Young convinced the Utes and Paiutes that the Mormons were their friends and that the Gentiles were their enemies.

On the morning of September 8, 1857, the Fancher party left Cedar City and sought refuge in a valley to the southwest. They decided to stay a few days to rest and prepare for the difficult final leg of their journey.

As the men, women, and children of the wagon train sat down to eat breakfast, they were attacked. Shots ripped through the wagons and emigrants fell. Through the screams and the bullets, Fancher managed to circle the wagons. He rallied the men, who quickly constructed barriers for defense. The women and children huddled in the center and prayed.

For four days and nights, the company held on, running dangerously low on ammunition and water. Then Mormon leader John D. Lee walked toward them with a white flag of truce. He blamed the Indians for the fighting, and said he and his men would escort the survivors to a safe place in Cedar City. Exhausted, the emigrants did what they were told. The first wagon to leave carried young children and anyone who was wounded. Behind them walked women and older children. Farther behind, single file, several feet apart, each man of the company was escorted by a Mormon militiaman with a gun.

As the women and older children disappeared over a small hill, someone yelled. On this signal, each Mormon turned and shot the man next to him. In the blood bath that followed, everyone who was old enough to tell the story, including the women and children, were murdered.

Only the youngest, under six years of age, were spared. A member of the attacking Mormon militia, Bishop Phillip Klingensmith, found the wagon full of young children and calmed the hysterical horses. He told the screaming children he would protect them. He drove the wagon away, leaving the executioners behind to retrieve the valuables carried by the company and to hastily bury the dead.

Many children later said they remembered details of the massacre. But none of them knew who was responsible. The Mormon account was that the Indians attacked the wagon train first, and the Mormon militia sent a courier asking Brigham Young for advice. After the first Indian attack, the Mormons said they had sent for Lee, who had experience negotiating with the Indians. Lee said he had warned Mormon leaders that the Indians were determined. He swore that when he encountered the Fancher company, it was already under siege, and that he wept before the Indian leaders, begging for mercy for the emigrants.

However, some of the surviving children remembered that the "Indians" wore boots. Some saw Mormons washing war paint from their faces afterwards.

While the first group of attackers may have been Indian, it is clear Mormons finished the job. No one knows who gave the final order.

Bishop Klingensmith found homes for the surviving children. Some were cared for by families of men involved in the massacre. Two years later, a United States Indian agent tracked down seventeen of the eighteen surviving children and returned them to relatives in Arkansas. Ironically, their caretakers were paid for their services.

After the massacre, some of the Mormon leaders involved in the incident disappeared for a time. They would resurface, then go into hiding again when United States government investigators got too close. Phillip Klingensmith was caught first. He confessed in Pinoche, Nevada, in 1872. In court, he claimed he was afraid the Mormon militia would kill him had he not participated in the massacre. Klingensmith eventually left the Mormon church. Some say he was killed for breaking his oath of silence and telling about the massacre.

Authorities finally captured John D. Lee in 1874. Tried twice, he was the only Mormon convicted of the crime. His first trial in Beaver ended in a hung jury; four Mormons voted for acquittal and four non-Mormons favored conviction. In 1876, Lee was tried again in Salt Lake City with an all-Mormon jury. Negotiations between the federal government and territory of Utah determined that the court should not try to uncover the whole story or discover who else may have been to blame. Its task was to decide whether or not Lee had stepped outside of his responsibilities and committed murder. He was convicted.

Lee's execution took place at Mountain Meadow—the site of the massacre, and now part of Dixie National Forest. He was shot and his body was buried in Panguitch.

As happens in many cases of atrocity, those involved tried to forget. Mormons are encouraged to keep journals and remember the past. But, in this case, the events in a grassy southern Utah meadow went conspicuously unrecorded.

JOHNSTON MARCHES
AGAINST THE MORMONS

- 1858 -

WHEN REVEILLE SOUNDED AT 3 A.M. in the army camp, the soldiers sprang to life. They had been waiting almost a year for this day to arrive. After marching across the Great Plains and the Rocky Mountains, the men spent a long, cold winter at Fort Scott, Wyoming, on their way to confront the Mormons in Salt Lake City.

The stay at Fort Scott had been particularly miserable. Mormon militiamen sent by Brigham Young to slow the soldiers down had chased away their livestock and burned their wagons, leaving them little to eat. Later, as they marched down Echo Canyon, in the northern corner of Utah Territory, through clouds of dust so thick they became caked and unrecognizable, the soldiers cursed their "enemies" who were making this military campaign so detestable.

Then, within a day's march of the city, as the battalion climbed up Little Mountain and down Emigration Canyon, pure frustration fueled their footsteps. Their commander, Albert Sidney Johnston, had learned that a peace agreement had been reached—they were not to shoot anyone after all. After so many months of spoiling for a fight, they could only hope Johnston would refuse to enforce the cease-fire. The soldiers were at the mercy of a general's whim and a president's orders.

In May of 1857, President James Buchanan had decided to send an army of 2,500 men to install a governor of his choosing in Utah Territory. He expected the new governor, Alfred Cumming, to bring the Utah Territory back into line with the laws of the nation. If Cumming needed the U.S. Army, it would be at his side.

Many Americans agreed with the president's decision. They had heard that the Mormons were killing people on religious pretexts. Also, they were disgusted by the Mormon's widespread practice of polygamy (one man taking several wives). President Buchanan felt strongly that Mormon Church President Brigham Young was abusing his position as territorial governor, ignoring the U.S. Constitution's separation of church and state.

Brigham Young saw Buchanan's action as a declaration of war. He proclaimed martial law and called on all Mormons to prepare to defend themselves. The Mormons had already been expelled from their homes in Missouri and Illinois. They had come to Utah to find a safe haven. They did not want to move again.

Young prepared well for the arrival of the U.S. Army. He sent a ranger company of the Mormon militia under the command of Captain Porter Rockwell to delay the army on its westward trek. Using guerrilla tactics, Rockwell's militia succeeded in trapping the soldiers in Wyoming for the winter.

Next, Young ordered all Mormons to store grain and provisions for the coming conflict. He prohibited Mormons from selling anything to emigrants coming through the territory; the Mormons themselves would need everything they had. Many cached supplies in the mountains in case they had to take refuge there. And, each Mormon settlement raised a militia and prepared it for combat.

Finally, Young ordered all inhabitants of the northern Utah Territory to move south. They must leave nothing behind but boarded-up buildings. If the U.S. soldiers came through northern Utah, they would find no food, habitation, or grass to sustain them.

As the army approached Salt Lake City, it stopped at the mouth of Emigration Canyon on the ancient Lake Bonneville shoreline. There, Johnston's men paused to dust off their uniforms and shine their boots and bayonets. They looked down at the city they had come so far to fight—a green jewel in the desert, surrounded by mountains. They marveled at their first sight of civilization in almost a year. The tree-lined streets were laid out in a neat grid. The adobe houses wore fresh paint. At the outskirts of the city lay irrigated fields.

The soldiers formed ranks and marched down on Salt Lake City. They moved slowly along the streets, keeping time to the band's rendition of a drinking song, "One-Eyed Riley." Colonel Johnston led the way. The six-foot, two-hundred-pound man had thick brows and a steady, penetrating gaze. He was every inch a leader. On his right rode Philip St. George Cooke, who had reinforced Johnston's original army with his six companies of dragoons. Behind them rode the two peace commissioners, Lieutenant Colonel Charles Ferguson Smith, and mountain man–guide, Jim Bridger.

Johnston's army continued to pour out of the mountains. Colonel Edmund Brooke Alexander led ten units of infantry. A small battery of the Fourth Artillery rolled sluggishly after them. Next came Colonel Carlos Waite and those in his command, parts of the Fifth and Seventh Infantries. A short distance behind, the twenty-four howitzers of the Third Artillery rumbled down the road, stirring up billows of fine dust that obliterated the sun. Into the dust marched lines of grenadiers and horsemen and 250 mounted riflemen. Then came a mixed regiment made up of elements of the First Cavalry and Third and Sixth Infantries, led by Colonel William W. Loring. Finally, Captain Barnard Bee headed up a phalanx of volunteers: four companies of teamsters, some herders, and miles and miles of livestock.

After a time, the Mormon territorial militia came forward to meet the invading army. The Mormon horsemen, silver shining on their saddles, rode wordlessly around the army and disappeared. The U.S. troops cursed silently; the urge was strong to fight this outnumbered company of Mormons. But Johnston's army advanced without incident through the city, flags flying and band playing. Up and down the ranks, the marching and music filled the soldiers with pride. Their steps grew jauntier. The miles they had marched to reach this point melted away. They were on parade in the Mormon capital. They noticed that no one was watching. Except for a few men skulking behind the houses, the city was deserted. The soldiers felt as if they were marching through a town that had been decimated by drought or plague.

Handsome gray adobe houses sat quietly behind poplars, maples, shrubs, and neat fences. Shiny red cherries hung tantalizingly close to the road. Not a single chimney gave a welcoming wave of smoke. Most of the windows and doors were boarded up. Here and there, the blank eye of a curtainless window looked down on the marchers.

The soldiers stared at the empty houses. They had heard that some Mormon men married more than one wife and that each gable on a house signified another wife or family. To soldiers who had been without home or family for more than a year, this Mormon practice represented an ungodly bounty. But where were the women and children? The lurking men carried pistols and clubs, and seemed to be leering at the soldiers. Those dark faces covered with large hats exemplified every awful, debased thing they had heard about Mormons. But the few they saw added up to an awfully small army to fight.

What the soldiers might not have noticed were the scattered piles of straw. Every earthly possession the fleeing Mormons could not fit in their wagons was hidden under the straw. The men left behind had been instructed to light the straw rather than let the army have the goods. And if the army tried to move into the houses, those would be burned too. One family had meticulously buried their piano; after painstakingly hauling it across the country, they could not bear to think of it being put to the torch.

Colonel Robert T. Burton of the Mormon militia was hiding in Brigham Young's home, the Beehive House. From there, the Colonel and his men watched for signs of aggression and waited to give the orders to burn the city. Burton later said that Johnston's army had fallen silent by the time it reached the Beehive House.

Colonel Johnston and his peace commissioners led the troops down Brigham Street (now South Temple) past Temple Square. Work on the foundation of the Mormon Temple had been halted, and the workers had spread straw over it to make it look like a plowed field. Johnston halted his company at the mansion of a prominent businessman, William Staines, where he was greeted by the new governor of the territory, Alfred Cumming, and his wife. Brigham Young was nowhere to be seen.

An intermediary, Thomas L. Kane, had already brokered a deal between Brigham Young, Alfred Cumming, and President Buchanan. Kane and Alfred Cumming had met with Brigham Young. Cumming promised to house the army far enough from Salt Lake City for Young's comfort. Young officially agreed to submit to the authority of the President of the United States. He allowed himself to be forgiven for the treason he supposedly committed. Since, in his own mind, he had committed no treason, Young saw the amnesty as merely a means to peace.

Brigham Young knew the time for change had arrived. When he first came to the valley in 1847, Young had said he would need ten years of peace to build his kingdom. His ten years were up. Johnston's coming signaled the end of Mormon isolation. The United States government would now be involved in the Mormons' affairs, and in exchange, would legitimize and protect their existence.

Cumming explained the results of the negotiations to Johnston, and Johnston left the mansion. Reflecting the mood of his troops, he supposedly told an associate he "would give his plantation for a chance to bombard the city for fifteen minutes." Instead, he climbed back on his horse and led his army out of the city. The only sounds were those of the marching feet, the rolling wheels of wagons and artillery, and the shuffling and lowing of hundreds of cattle. The city's lush vegetation soon gave way to a sagebrush filled desert. The men marched on. Some collapsed in the heat.

At last, the soldiers crossed the Jordan River and stopped for the night in a grassy field. The next day, Johnston marched his army to the southwest. Near the small settlement of Fairfield, he established Camp Floyd. The camp was close enough to the major Mormon cities—Salt Lake City, Provo, and Fillmore—to respond to any problems the Mormons might cause, and far enough from Salt Lake City to avoid unnecessary conflicts.

Brigham Young took time to see that the peace agreement was being honored and that no other armies were marching against the Mormons. He then allowed his followers to return to their homes in the north.

Camp Floyd soon housed the largest troop concentration in the United States at the time, with a population of seven thousand. (Salt Lake City's population was about fifteen thousand.) Although Salt

Lake City's closed society was exposed to the "evils" of the outside world when the army arrived, it also benefited from the army's business. The soldiers spent most of their paychecks locally. When the Civil War broke out, the government ordered the camp closed and the soldiers sent elsewhere. The Mormons managed to buy $4 million worth of army surplus for $100,000.

Little remains of old Camp Floyd except for an inn that was run by Mormon John Carson and the old U.S. Army commissary. Both have been restored. The state of Utah manages the property as Stagecoach Inn State Park.

HOWARD EGAN'S RIDE
FOR THE PONY EXPRESS

- 1860 -

MAJOR HOWARD EGAN WAS A MAN OF PRINCIPLES and a man of action. As superintendent of the Pony Express route through Utah, he was not going to sit around waiting for a mistake to be made on the first Pony Express ride in history. His bosses had told him to do something he knew was wrong. He would find a way to do what was right.

The eyes of the nation watched the Pony Express's first run. People wanted to see how fast its riders could carry the mail from St. Joseph, Missouri, to Sacramento, California. At the time, the United States government had an exclusive and expensive contract with John Butterfield to carry government mail by stagecoach on a southern route. Egan and his bosses, Russell, Majors, and Waddell, wanted to get the contract away from Butterfield, and at the same time, generate a private mail business for themselves. To do it, they would have to prove the feasibility of this northern route in year-round weather and would have to prove that they were faster than Butterfield—much faster.

Mail service took twenty-one days or more by stagecoach or wagon train. Egan and the Pony Express riders wanted to shorten the time to ten days. To deliver the mail more quickly, riders would race the mail from both the eastern and the western ends of the route at the same time. One rider was assigned to two stops on each section of the route. For example, a rider would pick up eastbound mail in Rush Valley and take it to Salt Lake City. While another rider relayed that mail further east, the rider from Rush Valley would carry the westbound mail from Salt Lake City back to Rush Valley.

It seemed ridiculous, therefore, that Egan's bosses had given the order to change the regular procedure and keep two Pony Express riders in Salt Lake City instead of sending one to Rush Valley. The top men obviously didn't know the riders and the territory as well as Egan did. Moreover, Egan knew that a congratulatory message from President James Buchanan lay waiting in the westbound mail. It had arrived by telegraph at St. Joseph, Missouri. The Pony Express would carry it to California, and Egan wanted the message to get through as quickly as possible.

An explanation had come with his bosses' order, but Egan found it insufficient. Egan's superiors had guessed that the muddy roads and rugged mountains of California and Nevada would slow down the riders on the western end of the route. They figured the men who traveled over the flat Great Plains would make much better time, and therefore, the mail from the west would not reach Rush Valley by the time a rider arrived from the east. For this reason, they kept the Rush Valley rider in Salt Lake City to wait for another rider from the east with more westbound mail. He would then take the mail to Rush Valley to meet the western carrier, who would (the bosses assumed) arrive late.

Major Egan disagreed with his superiors. They underestimated his riders and overestimated the terrain. He had personally scouted the entire 300 miles of the route from Salt Lake City to Sacramento. He had even driven cattle and freight wagons over it. Pony Express horses could gallop at full speed over that route for 20 to 25 miles at a time. His horses ran the gamut from barely broken mustangs to thoroughbreds, but all of them were fast. Many of them came from a ranch not far from Salt Lake City.

Egan trusted his riders, too. They were young men, but they were experienced. Every one of them weighed less than 130 pounds and had taken an oath not to swear, drink hard liquor, or fight with others in the company. Every worker on the Pony Express route would do everything he could to ensure the timely arrival of the mail— including Egan.

Egan decided to demonstrate the quality of his men and horses to his bosses. He was certain the western riders were as fast as the eastern riders and he didn't want the mail sitting at a station waiting for a rider. If his bosses wouldn't send a rider, he would race to Rush Valley and pick up the mail himself. Confident and impatient, Egan set out from Salt Lake City to meet the mail in Rush Valley.

Most Pony Express riders traveled light. Their uniform was a buckskin shirt, cloth trousers tucked into high boots, and a slouch hat or cap. In the early days, each rider carried a knife, a pair of Colt revolvers in holsters around his waist, a Spencer rifle slung across his back, and a horn or whistle to announce his approach to a station. Later, the rifle, horn, and one revolver were eliminated in order to lighten the load.

Each station manager made sure he had a fresh horse saddled and ready to go for the incoming rider. During the day, a dust cloud announced a rider's arrival. At night, the rider would whoop or whistle as he approached the station.

Doc Faust was the station manager at Rush Valley. Doc had once studied medicine, but during the gold rush in California, he got sidetracked prospecting for gold. When prospecting hadn't worked out, Faust joined the Mormon Church and came to Utah. Now he worked the Rush Valley Station.

When Egan reached Rush Valley Station, he found William Fisher already there with the mail. Fisher had ridden 75 miles across the Great Basin desert in five hours. If Egan or another rider hadn't shown up, Doc Faust was ready to take the mail on to Salt Lake City himself. Egan had been right about the dedication of his men.

Fisher arrived in Rush Valley under stormy skies. Doc Faust carefully transferred the leather mochila carrying the mail from the tired horse to the fresh one. The mochila was a square piece of leather with four pockets for mail. It fit right down over the saddle horn so the rider could sit on it. The mail in the mochila was sorted geographically and locked into the pouches.

By the time Egan showed up to take the mail, the weather had worsened. As he rode east, darkness fell and a combination of rain and sleet pounded his face, blinding him. Egan listened intently. As long as he heard his horse's hooves hitting the trail, he knew he was okay. If the horse veered off into brush or mud, Egan would be in trouble.

Suddenly, the horse's hooves hit the planks of a bridge. In the dark, horse and rider plunged off the side into the river. The water reached up the horse's sides to Egan's knees. He struggled to hold on and help his horse cross the river. They made their way over, scrambled up the opposite bank, and raced on.

Egan rode up to the Salt Lake City Main Street Pony Express office late that night, much earlier than anyone had expected. Thanks to Egan's initiative and his dedicated riders, the mail had come in way ahead of schedule.

Egan carried eighty-five pieces of mail that April night. The heaviest load a mail pouch could carry was twenty pounds. Letter writers used tissue-thin paper. At five dollars each half-ounce, words were expensive and were kept to a minimum. The high price of postage meant that during its nearly nineteen months of service, the Pony Express's main customers were local governments, businesses, and newspapers. Russell, Majors, and Waddell never did win the federal mail contract from Butterfield—politics intervened.

Even though the Pony Express never carried much "regular" mail, its short history was significant. Many emigrant wagon trains and freight companies used Pony Express routes and rested at Pony Express stations. In addition, the Pony Express improved communication between government officials—a critical consideration in the weeks before and after the beginning of the Civil War. The *Deseret News* of Salt Lake City—nicknamed "The Pony Dispatch"—printed news received through Express riders. In this way, citizens heard about Lincoln's election in eight days instead of the usual six weeks.

The Pony Express closed its route in October of 1861 when telegraph lines joined the East Coast to the West through Salt Lake City. The Overland Mail used Major Egan's Deep Creek Station until 1869. Just to the north, at Promontory Summit, Utah, the completion of the transcontinental railroad put the Overland out of business too.

In its heyday, the Pony Express employed 80 riders and 400 station managers and assistants; it used 190 stations and 420 horses. With an average of 125 miles covered by each rider in a single day, the mail traveled 250 miles in 24 hours. Riders were paid relatively well, between $50 and $100 a month. For this, they braved snowstorms, hostile Indians, and other dangers.

The story of the Pony Express has inspired many Americans. The Pony Express Trail in Utah is well marked. Motorists and equestrians alike visit its stations all across the Great Basin.

JEAN BAPTISTE ROBS
SALT LAKE'S GRAVES

- 1862 -

HENRY HEATH HAD SERVED as a Salt Lake City police officer for a long while, but no case had ever made his skin crawl like this one. A dead man had been robbed—of his clothes!

Not long before, the town had buried Moroni Clawson. Out of pity, Henry had used his own money to buy burial clothes for Moroni. Now Moroni's brother was accusing him of burying the man naked. Wondering what could possibly have happened, Heath rode with four other men to the Salt Lake City Cemetery to investigate.

The Clawson affair was bigger than it seemed; it was all mixed up with Utah's territorial politics. A month earlier, President Abraham Lincoln had appointed John W. Dawson governor of Utah Territory. The reaction was not favorable. The majority of Mormons and their leader, Brigham Young, resented the federal government's intrusion into their lives, and they disliked Dawson.

Ever since his arrival in Salt Lake City, Dawson had been hard to work with. But the residents could not get rid of him. Eventually, after an embarrassing personal blunder, Dawson decided to leave town of his own accord. A certain widow in Salt Lake City loudly accused Dawson of making uninvited advances toward her. The territorial governor hopped the next stagecoach out of town.

A small group of men, including one of the widow's relatives, refused to let the insult rest. They followed the stage. At Hanks Station, near Little Dell, east of Salt Lake City, they dragged Dawson from the stage and beat him mercilessly. They also "liberated" his luggage.

The Mormons didn't like Dawson, but they needed to convince the skeptical eastern politicians that they were law-abiding citizens. They organized a posse to catch the scoundrels who had assaulted Governor Dawson. One of the culprits, Moroni Clawson, was killed by a policeman, Porter Rockwell, the next day while trying to escape.

At first, no one came forward to claim Clawson's body. Salt Lake County paid for his burial, and Officer Henry Heath bought the burial clothes. A few days later, Heath ran into Moroni's brother, George, who accused him of callously burying Moroni without clothes. George had discovered his brother's condition when he exhumed the body to rebury it at his home in Willow Creek. When Heath protested, saying Clawson was fully clothed, George called him a liar and demanded justice. Heath received permission from Judge Elias Smith to investigate the incident.

The policemen first interrogated the sexton of the cemetery, Colonel S. C. Little. Little seemed genuinely perplexed at their questions, so they decided to look in on the grave digger, Jean Baptiste. Baptiste had worked in Salt Lake City's cemetery for five years. A scrawny man who was seldom seen or heard, Baptiste was said to have come to America from Italy, via Australia. Most Salt Lake City people called him John the Baptist.

When police arrived at the small house on Third Avenue between P and R Streets, Baptiste was out. They tried to question his wife, but she acted strangely, and they decided she was half-witted. So they searched the room, examining a pile of boxes they found there. Inside the boxes were sixty pairs of children's shoes and piles of burial garments. Baptiste, it seemed, had been digging up those he buried and keeping their clothes!

Heath was seized with revulsion, anger, and panic. His own daughter was buried in the same cemetery, not far from Clawson. The police officers hurried from the house in search of Baptiste. They found him at the cemetery, digging. Heath demanded that Baptiste confess. The little man groveled in the dirt, swearing his innocence. Infuriated, Heath grabbed Baptiste by the neck and shook him. This time, Baptiste whimpered that he had dug up just a few graves.

Heath dragged Baptiste to the grave next to his daughter's. He demanded to know if Baptiste had opened it. Baptiste answered, "yes." Then Heath pointed to his daughter's grave and asked the same question. The miserable man said, "no," which probably saved his life.

Heath wanted to believe Baptiste, but from the contents of the boxes, investigators estimated the grave digger had robbed at least 300 graves. The next day, Baptiste was taken from the jail to the cemetery to point out the graves he had desecrated. He could only identify a dozen.

As soon as Baptiste was locked deep in the county jail, the city learned what had happened. The police disclosed that after Baptiste had dug up the dead and taken their clothes, he had used their coffins for kindling. Hundreds jammed the streets outside the jail, demanding to know if their loved ones were among Baptiste's victims. They wanted to get their hands on him.

The city was in turmoil. Mormon Church President Brigham Young stepped in to calm his followers. Addressing a crowd assembled in the Mormon Tabernacle, he said that Jean Baptiste's deed was so awful he could not even comprehend it. Hanging, shooting, or life in prison would be too good for Baptiste. Young preferred to exile the man to ensure he lived the rest of his life in pain and isolation.

Brigham told the crowd he had three sisters, two wives, several children, and numerous other family members in the cemetery. At the resurrection, he said, they would appear as glorious as they were the day they were laid to rest and that is how he would remember them.

Young counseled those who could not follow his example—those who wanted to be sure their loved ones were buried in garments and left undisturbed by future fiends—by unburying their loved ones, clothing them, and burying them again in their gardens. After time had passed and their fears had quieted, he suggested returning the coffins to the cemetery.

No record of the case against Jean Baptiste, or of who decided it, exists. Judge Elias Smith recorded in his journal that he conducted a hearing for Baptiste, but he makes no mention of a trial.

Witnesses say the words "grave robber" were written on his forehead in indelible ink, and he was taken to Antelope Island in the middle of the Great Salt Lake. From that point, a pair of brothers were enlisted to ferry the prisoner to a more remote island in the lake, which they owned and which was surrounded by deep water. The island was named Miller Island after the two brothers. (It was later renamed Frémont Island after explorer John C. Frémont.) The Millers grazed cattle on the island and visited it every three weeks. They would keep Baptiste supplied with food and check on him regularly. He would stay in a small shack by himself. A small brackish spring would help keep him alive.

When he heard that he would be allowed to live, Baptiste was effusive in his thanks. He didn't mind dealing with the dead, but he was terrified of death. His thoughts on being deposited at the island are lost. Frémont Island is small; it can be traversed in a couple of hours. Its rocky outcroppings host gulls, pelicans, and a few lizards and snakes. Its barren slopes are blazing hot in the summer and frightfully cold in the winter. Baptiste could hardly have been delighted with his new home.

During their first visit to the island, the Miller brothers found Baptiste alive in the shack. The next time they came, he was missing. The roof and one side of the shack were also gone. The brothers found a slaughtered heifer nearby. Baptiste had apparently used strips of its hide to fasten the lumber together into a raft.

On the Great Salt Lake, the wind can come up at any time and whip up waves so salty they strangle people who swallow the water. Baptiste could easily have drowned. If he had returned to civilization, surely someone would have noticed the indelible mark on his forehead. In fact, some claimed to have seen him in Montana, or maybe in California. One man found a skeleton with a ball and chain on its leg bone in the Jordan River, a tributary to the Great Salt Lake. Some suggested it was Baptiste's. Yet there was no record that he was left on the island wearing a ball and chain.

Baptiste had disappeared into the lake and into legend.

DRIVING THE GOLDEN SPIKE

- 1869 -

SITTING IN THE MIDST OF UTAH'S NORTHWESTERN DESERT, desolate Promontory Summit gives little indication that it is one of the most significant sites in the history of the United States. Little about the place has changed since this 1869 account: "The town consists of a few tents, the ticket houses of both companies, their telegraph offices, hordes of grasshoppers and swarms of sand fleas."

Yet, at 12:47 P.M. on May 10, 1869, history was made at Promontory Summit when a golden spike was driven through a tie to complete the first transcontinental railroad in the United States.

The country would never be the same, and those at Promontory Summit that morning knew it. Travelers could now ride from New York to California in six days and twenty-two minutes. Before the two rail lines connected, travel from Independence, Missouri, to Sacramento, California, took six months by wagon train. Businessmen could now ship grain or cattle to markets on either coast quickly and easily. Settlers would soon fill in the vast spaces in the West and would stimulate business with their needs for goods and services.

The railroad magnates, Central Pacific's Leland Stanford and Union Pacific's Thomas Durant, had plenty to celebrate. They had overcome many obstacles, Congress's bickering not the least among them. Despite the turmoil of the Civil War, the railroaders had persuaded their legislators to authorize the building of the transcontinental line.

The project began in 1863. Stanford's Central Pacific Railroad had started in California, laying track eastward from Sacramento. The Union Pacific Railroad headed west from Omaha. Congress gave each railroad ten alternate sections of land and subsidized loans of between $16,000 and $48,000 for each mile of track.

The men who actually built the railroad were a mixed population; their demographics reveal much about American society in the 1860s. Irish, German, and Italian immigrants joined ex-Civil War veterans from both sides of the conflict along with freed slaves to work for the Union Pacific. The mixture of races, nationalities, and loyalties among soldiers made this an interesting group that did not get along easily.

The Central Pacific imported ten thousand Chinese laborers to build its tracks. The terrain—which included the Sierra Nevada Mountains and the scorching Great Basin Desert—was difficult at best. To complicate matters further, all the Central Pacific's materials, including rails, spikes, and locomotives, had to be shipped 15,000 miles around Cape Horn.

Many people compromised to bring about the celebration at Promontory Summit that morning. As the two railroads neared completion, they passed each other without connecting tracks. Bickering and profiteering led to building more than 200 miles of railroad on nearly parallel grades. Congress finally intervened, ordering the rails to be joined at Promontory Summit on May 10, 1869.

Some early newspaper stories said the rails would be joined at Promontory Point, a spot about 35 miles away from Promontory

Summit. To this day, many Utahns and even some American history textbooks perpetuate the myth of Promontory Point.

The plans for the celebration underwent change and compromise too. Neither of the locomotives that brought Durant and Stanford to the historic spot—the Central Pacific's *Jupiter* and the Union Pacific's *119*—were scheduled to star in the big occasion.

Leland Stanford had planned to arrive in a train pulled by a special locomotive called the *Antelope*. As Stanford's locomotive approached its destination, railroad workers failed to notice the small green flag that signaled the arrival of another train, and they had rolled a log down the cut near the tracks. The *Antelope* hit the log and was too damaged to use. Railroad officials elected to couple the Central Pacific dignitaries' cars to a regular engine. The substitute engine, *Jupiter,* took the *Antelope*'s place in the famous photo of the "Wedding of the Rails" snapped by Andrew J. Russell.

The Union Pacific also pressed a substitute locomotive into service in the last hours of the adventure. History doesn't record the name of the engine that should have brought Durant to Promontory Summit, but the combination of a rickety wooden bridge and the swollen Weber River knocked the chosen locomotive out of the running. That engine was far too heavy to safely cross the bridge at Devils Gate, east of Ogden, so the cars carrying Durant and his party were detached from the engine and pushed across the bridge. Once the cars were safely on the other side, the *119* picked them up and transported them to the historic meeting site. (The bridge was strengthened later for regular railroad traffic.)

The celebration itself was lengthy and awkward. The dignitaries gave interminable speeches, congratulating themselves on achieving the historic linkage. Durant, apparently still recovering from the party the night before, left the group for a short time. Grenville Dodge, the Union Pacific's chief engineer, stepped in to give Durant's speech. Durant later returned to finish the ceremony.

The workers watched as two golden spikes were presented to Stanford, who dropped them into the first and fourth predrilled holes in a laurelwood tie. Durant put a silver spike donated by the State of Nevada and a gold-silver-iron-alloy spike donated by the State of Arizona in the other two holes. The precious metal spikes and laurelwood tie were then removed and replaced with a regular tie and four iron spikes.

At the proper moment, the dignitaries were supposed to drive in the final iron spike. This spike was wired to the telegraph. Three ticks on the telegraph would signal to the whole country that the railroad was finished. But the "big men" of the railroad, who were used to wielding fountain pens instead of mauls, kept missing the mark. The workers rolled with laughter.

James Strobridge, supervisor of the Chinese construction crews, finally drove in the last spike. The telegraph operator sent a simple four-letter message—D-O-N-E. At long last, the transcontinental railroad had been completed. Together, railroad crews from the Union Pacific and Central Pacific Railroads crossed 1,776 miles of rugged and often hostile terrain. The United States was united by rail for the first time.

These days, exact replicas of the *Jupiter* and the *119* puff out of their engine house at the Golden Spike National Historic Site (managed by the National Park Service) during the summer months; at other times of the year, visitors view the locomotives inside a large garage. A reenactment ceremony occurs annually on May 10. A variety of films, exhibits, hikes, and interpretive drives celebrate the joining of the rails.

LONG JOHNS SAVE
JOHN WESLEY POWELL

- 1869 -

JOHN WESLEY POWELL FOUND HIMSELF in a difficult spot. On July 8, 1869, the leader of the first expedition down the Green and Colorado Rivers had set out to climb to the top of Desolation Canyon above the Green River. As he held on and waited for help, Powell knew he would be lucky to make it down to the river in one piece.

Powell's climbs always frustrated the nine other men who had joined the one-armed Civil War veteran to explore the 1,200 miles of river between Green River, Wyoming, and the end of the Grand Canyon in Nevada. Though they were in a hurry to get down the river, Powell insisted on collecting information on all aspects of the river, including its canyon walls. His sponsor, the United States government, had instructed him to map the area and collect scientific data on the unexplored region. A geologist and one of the nation's first authorities on irrigation, Powell felt obligated and personally compelled to learn as much as possible about this arid region.

The men of the expedition worried about every possible disaster. Many had already befallen them. Earlier in the trip, in Colorado, one of the expedition's four boats—the *No Name*—crashed into a rock in Lodore Canyon. The boat and a portion of the food rations were lost. Powell named the place "Disaster Falls." Soon after that, while still in Lodore Canyon, fire ravaged one of the party's camps. In his rush to board a boat to escape, the cook had dropped many of his utensils into the river. Rations were short, and the men wanted to reach the end of the long and dangerous exploration before their food ran out.

In Desolation Canyon, they found themselves in the middle of another unbelievable disaster. Their leader had put himself—and all of them—in danger. George Bradley and his long johns were the only hope they had.

Before they took to the boats that morning, Powell had insisted on taking a barometric reading so he could calculate the height of the cliffs. He also wanted to take notes on the area surrounding the top of the canyon. Bradley had accompanied Powell on the climb. Having surveyed the steep canyon walls carefully, the pair thought they had mapped out a secure route to the top. From the river's edge they picked their way upward through a gulch to a ledge. Scrambling up boulders and through crevices, they climbed from bench to bench. Yet as they worked their way up the side of the cliff, it became more difficult to keep to the route they had chosen. Toward the top, 600 to 800 feet from the river, Bradley and Powell thought they could go no further. The wall seemed smoother, with fewer footholds. They searched for notches or protruding rocks. Finally, they settled on a route. Upward they climbed, one precarious foothold after another.

Powell was at a disadvantage when climbing in this manner. As a U.S. Army major at the Battle of Shiloh in the Civil War, he had raised his right arm to order his men to fire and lost it above the elbow when a mini-ball hit it. His disability had not stopped him from becoming a college professor or gaining the backing for his expeditions. It had not inhibited his guiding their wooden dories down the Green River. This time, however, he had a problem.

Roughly 200 feet below the summit, he had jumped, placing one foot in a crack and grabbing a rock over his head. From this position, however, he found he had no more footholds above him. If he let go to drop back to his previous spot, chances were he would slide off the ledge and fall 60 to 80 feet to the next ledge or farther.

Powell yelled to Bradley below him. He needed help. Muscles trembling, Powell clung to the cliff with fingers and toes. Bradley worked his way around and above Powell. From a ledge over Powell's head, but out of reach, Bradley searched for a branch he could hand down to Powell. Finding none, he suggested Powell let go of the rock and grab the barometer case. Powell declined. The case's cover was too smooth. Seconds passed. Finally, Bradley had an idea. To make their outer clothing last longer, members of the expedition had taken to wearing only their woolen long johns. After being wet for days on end, the sleeves and legs would stretch out and the men would cut them off. Bradley yelled to Powell that he would use his long johns like a rope. Quickly, Bradley took off his drawers and dangled them down to Powell. Powell leaned into the rock, let go with his hand, and grabbed the long johns. Bradley hoisted him up to his ledge.

Together, the men made their way up the final stretch to the top of Desolation Canyon. From this vantage point, 1,000 feet above the river, they saw miles and miles of the same rugged country. Powell made his scientific calculations, and they found an easier way down.

Later, Bradley and Powell both described this adventure in their journals. While they recorded the event at different dates and places, descriptions of Bradley's use of his long johns are much the same. Powell's published journal, *The Exploration of the Colorado River and Its Canyons* contains a combined account of both his 1869 and 1871 trips down the Colorado and Green Rivers and more details of Bradley's heroic long john rescue. Neither man would ever forget the near fatal ascent of the canyon.

River historian Roy Webb calls the Powell expedition "one of America's last great geographic explorations." What saved John Wesley Powell from serious injury or death, allowing his expedition to reach its triumphant conclusion in the Grand Canyon? George Bradley's quick thinking and his long johns.

ARSENAL HILL EXPLODES

- 1876 -

FRANK HILL AND CHARLES RICHARDSON LOOKED innocent enough. No one would guess they were capable of causing mass destruction. Wandering home after a day of herding cattle in the foothills of Salt Lake City, the boys chattered and joked. They looked down at the valley spread out before them. A cold April wind blew up City Creek Canyon, tugging at their clothes. The sound of cheers and yells floated up from a group of boys playing ball on the Deseret baseball field. Having seen wild chickens on the hill the day before, Charles brought along a rifle thinking he would take a crack at them.

When they reached the powder magazines on Arsenal Hill, the boys paused. In the 1860s the Mormons had stored all of their military firearms in a warehouse there (thus it was given the name "Arsenal Hill"). The warehouse had been used as a slaughterhouse before it burned down. It remained a deadly place. Several businesses in town kept gunpowder and explosives for sale in buildings on the hill. The stockpile included forty tons of black powder, two tons of blasting caps, and sticks of some of the most destructive blasting powder around, Hercules.

The four brick-and-stone buildings, set close together, had tin roofs and iron doors. The doors attracted the boys' attention. They were tempting targets for amateur marksmen. The iron was already pockmarked with bullet holes. Frank and Charles glanced around; they were far from town and alone.

The boys playing baseball heard rifle shots, looked up, and saw Charles and Frank. Then the first powder magazine exploded. Within forty-two seconds, three more magazines ignited. Forty-five tons of explosives scattered about five hundred tons of rock, brick, and debris over a 1½ mile radius. The ground shook. A billowing cloud of dust arose from the craters. Debris knocked some of the boys on the baseball team unconscious. Others took cover behind the old city wall and then ran for home.

No one else knew what was happening. The Mormon Church's annual spring conference had brought visitors from all over the territory to Salt Lake City. Many people thought it was an earthquake or a volcano. Some Latter-day Saints believed the judgment day had come. Shards of flying glass and rocks—some the size of peas, others as big as small dogs—sprayed the north side of the city. Horses panicked and bolted. Buildings swayed. People fainted, prayed, and waited for the sky to stop falling.

When it did, they went looking for the cause. There, on Arsenal Hill, they found the craters where the powder magazines had stood. They also found what was left of Charles and Frank. The pieces were taken to city hall for their parents to claim.

Other victims were also identified. Mary Jane Vanatta had been pumping water from a neighbor's well, ¾ of a mile from the blast. She was killed when a rock hit her back. A few blocks away, a rock tore through a three-year-old boy. It was said another woman died of fright. Surprisingly, no one else died in the chaos. The survivors prayed many thankful prayers that day. The cold, unfriendly weather had kept people inside, probably saving many lives.

Many people suffered near-misses. The explosion threw Mrs. E. L. T. Harrison from her chair. She and her baby, seriously injured by flying glass, survived. Another woman grabbed her baby from its cradle after the first blast and ran outside. When she went back inside, she found the cradle crushed by fallen debris. Two men in Shingleton's Saloon stared in disbelief as a 115-pound boulder crashed through the ceiling, then through the floor right next to them, and down into the cellar before finally burrowing four feet into the earth.

The property damage was tremendous. Homeowners found broken locks, cracked walls, and shattered dishes. Windows everywhere were in pieces. The wooden roof over the water reservoirs in City Creek Canyon collapsed. Brigham Young's Empire Flour Mill in the canyon was picked up off its foundation and smashed. The miller survived; he was loading flour sacks on a wagon outside and was thrown clear of the mill.

The Mormon Church's annual conference went on. The attendees shivered in the Tabernacle, the main Mormon meeting house. Brigham Young's followers had draped cloth over the thousand missing windowpanes, but they couldn't keep out the frigid air. Young himself came down with a cold and missed the last two days of meetings.

Broken glass littered the city, causing much concern. Workers carted wheelbarrow loads of shards and pieces away to the dump. As the repairs began, glass dealers combed the territory for supplies. Some grumbled that the price of glass had risen, but the dealers insisted it hadn't.

The hill above the city was still a danger zone. Unexploded Hercules powder sticks were scattered everywhere. City officials had a hard time securing the area around the blast site. Curious residents who went up the hill to investigate were handling the highly sensitive explosives. Newspaper stories screamed at citizens to stay away from Arsenal Hill. Even more problematic for the general public were the sticks of Hercules powder that kept showing up in yards and gardens in the weeks after the accident.

That is what the explosion on Arsenal Hill was called—an accident. At the inquest, a coroner's jury decided that a wad of burning paper from a rifle had ignited loose powder around the powder magazine.

Meanwhile, city officials were occupied in solving another problem. A large shipment of explosives was on its way to Salt Lake City, and there was no place to put it. The leaders decided to build new powder magazines on the bench area northeast of Warm Springs, around the hill from the old ones. The new site was close to the railroad. The explosives could be transferred from the trains to wagons and transported to the new magazines on city streets.

Those living near the new site protested loudly. They organized and circulated petitions. But the powder magazines were built. The owners assured the public that the new design was foolproof. The buildings had 13-inch-thick outer walls, 3 inches of air space, and 4 inches of inner wall. The roofs were galvanized sheet iron, and the double iron doors were five-sixteenths of an inch thick.

Salt Lake City leaders passed a stricter explosives ordinance. Extensive newspaper coverage of the blast outside the state prompted other cities to look at their explosive storage plans and make their cities safer.

Life soon returned to normal in Salt Lake City. The new powder magazines blended into the landscape. As the city grew larger, the buildings were removed. Today, the Utah State Capitol sits slightly to the south of the place where two boys blew up Arsenal Hill.

DESCENT THROUGH
THE HOLE-IN-THE-ROCK

- 1880 -

THEY HAD CROSSED THE OCEAN. They had crossed the Great Plains. They had fought religious persecution, hunger, thirst, cold, and fear. And now this. Even the most devout Mormon pioneer must have felt a twinge of doubt as to God's—or at least their leaders'—wisdom. The group of men and women craned their necks to see down the Hole-in-the-Rock. In 1 short mile, the trail dropped 1,800 feet. The pioneers must surely have questioned the sanity of the scouts who had reported the crevice as passable by wagons.

Mormon Church President John Taylor had called on a group of pioneers to colonize remote Montezuma Creek. Eventually, 236 intrepid pioneers in eighty-two wagons undertook the journey. Some of the families had arrived in Utah recently. Most of them had only just settled in Cedar City and Parowan when their church leaders asked them to move again to the rugged southeastern edge of the territory.

They knew that to get there they must pass through the crack in the cliff called Hole-in-the-Rock.

Leader Silas Stanford Smith and his company had chosen this route as a shortcut to save them 250 miles. By the time the party reached the eastern edge of Glen Canyon, on the Colorado River, in the middle of December, they were beyond the point of no return. Snow blanketed the mountains behind them, preventing a retreat.

The travelers took one look at the crack in the canyon wall and decided Smith and his two boys would head back to Salt Lake City. Smith would talk the Territorial Legislature (of which he was a past member) and Church authorities into allocating money for blasting powder and other equipment the pioneers needed. Leaving Platte Lyman in charge, Smith set off on a nine-day winter trek. He caught pneumonia, but sent back 1,025 pounds of blasting powder and $500 worth of food and supplies.

To spread out the impact on the desert's supply of water and livestock forage, Platte Lyman decided to settle half the pioneers in a camp 5 miles from the edge of Glen Canyon and the other half at the edge. The men from the remote camp would walk to the edge to work and live during the week, returning to their families on Saturday night.

The Hole-in-the-Rock trail dropped over two cliffs and a long sand dune. Three groups of men worked simultaneously on different parts of the trail to make it passable for the wagons. The first group attacked the initial 45-foot drop. Dangling from ropes in half barrels, the men chiseled holes and inserted blasting powder. They blasted out a giant block of solid sandstone, widened the crack, and made the grade less steep.

The next group tried another method of road building on the second cliff. Instead of blasting the rock away to make a ledge, they would attach a road onto the rock wall. Working below the first group, brothers Benjamin and Hyrum Perkins and Jens Nielson were held from the cliff by ropes. They blasted a small ledge for the uphill wagon wheels. Beneath this small ledge, they drilled holes 18 inches apart into which they inserted stakes. Across the stakes, they placed cottonwood poles. Upon this base, they made a roadbed of rocks and brush for the downhill wheels. In this manner, they constructed a 50-foot-long road coming out almost perpendicular to the wall. This part of the trail was named Uncle Ben's Dugout after Benjamin Perkins whose engineering expertise was critical to the effort.

A third team set to work at the base of the Hole-in-the-Rock, building a boat to ferry the wagons, two at a time, across the Colorado River. From there they could continue on to Montezuma Creek.

The men labored through cold, bitter days and even blizzards. On January 25, after three weeks, the trail down the Hole-in-the-Rock was complete. Despite all the pioneers' work, the view down the crack remained daunting. Elizabeth Morris Decker wrote to her parents, "If you ever come this way it will scare you to death to look down at it. It is about a mile from the top down to the river and it is almost straight down. The cliffs on each side are 500 feet high and there is just room enough for a wagon to go down."

When the time had come to start down, the leading team of horses reared into the air and lunged backwards, refusing to take the first steps. Many claimed to have been driving that first wagon, but the majority of accounts say it belonged to Benjamin Perkins, the man who dreamed up the floating road. Some accounts also say the pioneers finally got that first wagon down by using Joe Barton's horses. Blinded by pinkeye a year earlier, Barton's horses couldn't see how terrible the drop was. Fearlessly and slowly they led the way so the other horses would follow. Still, some stalled at the edge and had to be nudged off by men pushing the wagons from behind.

Pioneers devised several methods of keeping the wagons from going downhill too fast. They wrapped chains around the wheels and wagon box or running gears—like brakes—so that the wheels could not turn. They tied long ropes to the rear axles; ten or more men followed each wagon, holding onto the ropes and digging in their heels. The pioneers tried using horses for this job, but the animals got yanked off their feet and dragged. Danielson B. Barney tied two large juniper trees to the back of his wagon. Someone else used a large stake at the top of the crevice to anchor a pulley system.

The first wagons down had the easiest time. The loose rock and debris used to level the road slowed them down. But the passing of each wagon scoured the rock smoother.

Most women and children chose to walk down rather than ride in the wagons. Nathaniel Z. Decker marveled at "How mother and the rest of the kiddies got down without harm. I suppose they were too scared to get hurt. I could hardly keep my feet under me it was so steep and slick."

The last wagon of the day belonged to Joseph Stanford Smith. He had worked all day helping the first thirty-nine wagons down the Hole-in-the-Rock and onto the ferry, only to discover his own family and wagon deserted at the top. Leaving their two young children and baby alone up there, Smith and his wife, Belle, struggled to get their wagon down the grade. Belle took the rear ropes and pulled back on their old horse and the rear of the wagon. Meanwhile, her husband guided the front two horses. As the horses descended, Belle was thrown off her feet. She held on, and was dragged and thrown about; she made it to the bottom with a serious gash along her leg. On a rock above, a piece of her dress waved in the breeze, a flag of her bravery. When Belle and her husband hiked back up for the children, Joseph coldly met other members of the company who came too late to help. He didn't need them, he said. He had Belle.

The second group made its descent the next day. With no loss of life or wagons, and injuries no worse than cuts and bruises, the pioneers considered the Hole-in-the-Rock leg of the expedition a success. Beyond the Colorado River lay 150 miles of what Elizabeth Morris Decker called "nothing in the world but rocks and holes, hills and hollows." The mountains were "just one solid rock as smooth as an apple."

The trek the party had expected to take six weeks took six months, and the pioneers never made it as far as Montezuma Creek. Exhausted, they stopped short in a place they named Bluff City. Life was not easy in Bluff City. The water supply was inconsistent, and the farms never prospered. Many pioneers moved away.

Wagons going east and west used the Hole-in-the-Rock trail for years, until someone found a better route. As that first group of pioneers worked on the trail, they carved their names in the sandstone of the cliffs and into history.

A POLYNESIAN PIONEER DAY
IN IOSEPA

- 1892 -

As THEY WERE FERRIED ACROSS THE DESERT to the Polynesian settlement, the only waves the visitors saw were shimmering mirages. They
did not come by ship, but traveled in buggies and carriages or by
train. And they arrived at a different kind of island—a band of green
in the midst of the Great Basin's sagebrush desert. People had traveled from many parts of the Utah Territory to celebrate Pioneer Day
with the Polynesians.

Their hosts, mostly Hawaiian, had left their Pacific island homes
to come to Utah as Mormon converts. Like many converts, they
wanted to be near the heart of their church, the Mormon Temple,
where many important religious ceremonies were performed. A
group of fifty Polynesians had settled near Salt Lake City in what is
now the Beck Hot Springs area.

But the Polynesians had not been happy in the city. Differences
in culture and customs made it difficult for them to live surrounded

by white Mormons. So Mormon leaders helped the converts find a place to start a settlement of their own: Skull Valley. Seventy-five miles southwest of Salt Lake City, the valley was desolate and remote. The Goshute Indians had lived there, but most of them had been forced onto reservations. The Polynesians moved in, naming their settlement Iosepa after Joseph F. Smith, the man who had converted many of their congregation to Mormonism. (Iosepa is the Hawaiian spelling and pronunciation of Joseph.)

In three years, the Polynesians created an oasis of green in the middle of the Great Basin. The arrival of their guests signaled the beginning of a weekend celebrating their accomplishments. Most Mormon pioneers celebrate Pioneer Day on July 24, the day the first Mormons entered the Salt Lake Valley. The Church had designated August 28, the day the Polynesians entered Skull Valley, as a special Polynesian Pioneer Day.

The hundred visitors who approached Iosepa at dusk on Friday, August 26, were greeted with their first taste of Hawaiian hospitality. Men with torches stationed every 3 miles in the desert lit their way. Fires and fireworks lit up the liberty pole in the city center. Chinese lanterns glowed in the streets, and music filled the air.

Most of the visitors knew the Polynesians, either from their Mormon missionary work on the islands or from interactions in the territory. Mormon leaders and their wives and neighbors traveled from nearby Grantsville and Tooele. A few Goshute Indians came to take part in the festivities. While the hosts showed their guests to their quarters to freshen up and take care of their luggage, the Young Ladies' Glee Club and the Men's Mandolin and Guitar Club serenaded them. That night, the visitors forgot the dust and desert and fell asleep in comfort on a serene Polynesian island.

Because this particular Pioneer Day fell on a Sunday, the celebration unfolded somewhat differently. The usual parade of dignitaries,

Indians, and citizens through town would not be appropriate on the Sabbath.

On Saturday, the guests assembled at 10 A.M. on a platform with seats that had been constructed in a shady spot. After the band and choir performed, Iosepa President Harvey H. Cluff gave an official welcome and chaplain Peter Kesiakeikonus led a prayer. President Cluff was one of the few whites living in Iosepa, and he held an interesting position in addition to his presidency. The Mormon Church had helped the Polynesians purchase the land for their settlement, forming the Iosepa Agriculture and Stock Company. Cluff ran the company and employed the Polynesians. He was also their spiritual leader.

Joseph F. Smith addressed the guests in Hawaiian. He had gone to Hawaii at the age of fifteen and had known many of the Iosepans there. Next, several Mormon leaders and Utah Territorial Delegate John T. Caine gave speeches. In between speeches, the Polynesians entertained their guests. Hawaiian Brother Nihi had trained the Men's Mandolin and Guitar Club and the Young Ladies' Glee Club well. The women were clothed in the colors of their adopted country, with white blouses and skirts of red, white, and blue. Their caps had bands made of peacock feathers and were topped with red, white, and blue bunting.

After the benediction, the chaplain invited everyone to the bowery for a feast, encouraging the visitors to sample Hawaiian food. Central to the feast was the roast pig, cooked underground with many vegetables. Specially wrapped fish steamed on platters. In ponds they had created, the Polynesians raised carp and grew a substitute for seaweed. They wrapped their food in corn husks instead of the ti leaves native to Hawaii. They had also learned how to cook American dishes. Cakes, rice puddings, and platters of peaches and grapes from their gardens adorned the tables.

Poi was another essential element of the meal. Traditionally made from taro root, which would not grow in the Great Basin, American poi was made from flour and cornstarch. The Hawaiians poured these ingredients into boiling water and stirred them until they were smooth. They then strained the mixture through a flour sack and put it into an earthen jar to ferment. After fermentation, the poi was pounded on a flat board with a big ball stick until it became smooth and puffy like ice cream. The Hawaiians and their visitors ate the poi with their fingers in place of bread.

Although some visitors found the poi too strong for their taste, the consensus was that the food was delicious. The feast showed how hard the Polynesians had worked to recreate their lush homeland in the midst of a desert, and how successful they had been at farming. That year, in the midst of a depression in Utah, they had produced 650 tons of hay; 2,305 bushels of oats; 2,120 bushels of barley; 1,350 bushels of wheat; 250 bushels of corn; 177 bushels of potatoes; 100 tons of squash; 15 tons of beets; 1 ton of lucerne seeds; 10 tons of corn fodder; and a great quantity of vegetables, all worth between $7,000 and $8,000. An irrigation system that used water from the nearby Stansbury Mountains assisted in their agricultural success.

That afternoon, hosts and visitors met again to hear more speeches. The Glee Club, Mandolin and Guitar Club, and Grantsville Band entertained. When evening fell, the Iosepans showed off their Polynesian culture. Many performed songs and dances that represented ancient Hawaiian customs.

The next day, Sunday, the Mormons held their religious service. Joseph F. Smith spoke again, giving advice on how to live daily in a spiritual way and encouraging his audience to greater devotion.

The visitors left that afternoon, remarking on how prosperous and happy the settlement was. The Polynesians hoped they had communicated both their belief in Mormonism and the richness and importance of their Polynesian culture.

The settlement of Iosepa prospered until 1917. As in most pioneer settlements, the residents endured many hardships, including a few cases of leprosy. The town was not abandoned until the Mormon Church announced it would open a new temple in Laie, Oahu, Hawaii. Many Polynesians jumped at the chance to return to their island homes. Others had to be convinced it was a good idea. Ultimately, all but one family—the Hoopiiana brothers—left Utah.

Today, many Polynesians make their home in Utah. Their culture continues to enrich the state.

MARTHA HUGHES CANNON
WINS THE RACE

- 1896 -

MARTHA HUGHES CANNON HAD A GREAT DEAL RIDING on the 1896 election: years of hard work, her future, and perhaps her marriage. She and her husband were both running for the Utah state legislature. Fortunately, they weren't running head to head. Voters would elect five state senators out of a field of ten. So it was possible that both Martha and her husband, Angus Cannon, would win.

People thought it was nice that this husband and wife had politics in common. Angus was a Republican and Martha was a Democrat, but Martha and Angus respected each other and publicly supported each other's candidacy. Any way the election went, the public would be watching to see what happened between them. A woman running for office was sensational enough; how much more exciting to watch her run against her husband!

It was an interesting year in Utah politics. Utah had become a state the previous January. This was the first chance Utahns would have to vote for a President of the United States. The election for state senate was just as important. The state senators, not the public, would choose those who would represent Utah in the United States Senate.

If a woman running for office was unusual in the 1890s, so was the idea of women voting in elections. Nationally, women did not earn the right to vote until 1920. But Utah women had been voting since 1870—except for a nine year period when the United States government had taken the right away. Contrary to national practice, Utah included the women's right to vote in its state constitution. Utah women had been active in politics for a long time. Martha was not the only woman candidate in 1896; seven women were running for the Utah state legislature. The Democrat-Populist party and the Republican Party could each nominate five candidates for state senate. Martha was nominated by the Democratic-Populist convention to represent the twenty-second precinct of Salt Lake County. In his nominating speech for Martha, L. R. Letcher praised her as both a graduate of two medical colleges and a "womanly woman." He assured the voters that she would vote the party line and dared any man to vote against her. Martha garnered more votes than any other nominee at the convention. The Democratic Party felt it was important to show their support for women's suffrage.

Meanwhile, the Republican convention nominated Angus Cannon to run for state senate. For another of their five nominees, the Republicans also chose a woman, Martha's good friend and fellow suffragist, Emmeline B. Wells. Martha Cannon was in a tough spot, running against both her friend and her husband.

Martha was worried—not about her marriage, but about the election. She feared that voters would not want a husband and wife to work together and would vote for her husband instead of her. She knew also that many Gentiles (non-Mormons) would refuse to vote for her because she was a Mormon polygamist's wife.

Her husband could feel confident of his election because he was the Mormon state president in Salt Lake County, a prestigious and visible position. Cannon had six wives; Martha was his fourth. He had married Martha in 1884 in a secret ceremony because the federal government had begun to persecute polygamists. A few months after the marriage, federal agents caught up with Angus Cannon, and he had spent time in prison. Now, each of Angus's wives had her own household. Angus chose to live with none of them so the marshals could not arrest him again.

Martha and Angus had two children together. After the birth of her first child, Martha left the country to keep attention away from Angus. When the persecution of polygamists died down, Martha returned to Utah and immersed herself in the women's suffrage movement. She, Emmeline B. Wells, and others had worked to include women's right to vote in Utah's state constitution.

The 1896 campaign was long and hard. Martha traveled to Granger, Brigham City, South Taylorsville, Draper, the Third Municipal Ward, and even the Old Soldier's meeting to speak. Each speech exhorted citizens to vote Democratic. She asked for votes for her ideas, not her gender. Martha supported the Democratic candidate for President of the United States, William Jennings Bryan, over Republican William McKinley.

The hot national issue was the campaign for free coinage and silver. Both presidential candidate Bryan and the Utah Democratic Party were strongly opposed to the gold standard in the United States. The Republicans supported the standard. Martha promised, if she were elected, to vote for a senator who would oppose the gold standard in Congress.

The Utah Republican Party had split over the silver coinage debate. It cost them the election. Bryan carried Utah. The citizens didn't elect a single Republican to the state senate. Angus Cannon lost to former territorial representative, John T. Caine. Martha came in with the least number of votes in her party, but she won the race. She had received 2,671 more votes than Angus. Angus bore his disappointment well, saying he had always supported his wife.

Martha Hughes Cannon became the first woman state senator in the history of the United States. When a journalist asked how this made her feel, Martha replied that she had not thought much about her place in history, but she would have to try to live up to her privileges.

With Martha Cannon's notoriety, a spotlight was cast on her polygamous marriage. Many suffragists felt that polygamy was a plot by men to keep women enslaved. Martha countered that polygamy was an essential part of her religion, and she wished to live her faith fully. She also suggested that women who share their husband have more independence.

Health was a great interest of Senator Cannon's. She had spent most of her life training as a doctor and had received degrees in medicine and elocution. She met Angus while working as a resident physician at Deseret Hospital; he was on the board of directors. Martha had seen many women and children die because of the unhealthy condition of their lives. She was determined to do something about it.

As a freshman politician, Martha Cannon sponsored and passed three bills the first month. Senate Bill 31 improved the condition of women salesclerks; it mandated that stools or chairs be provided so the women would not have to stand all day. Senate Bill 22 allocated money for the education of sight- and hearing-impaired children. Senate Bill 27 created a Utah State Board of Health. The seven-member board would help establish local boards statewide that would improve sanitation, clean water supply, and control disease. The legislation Cannon introduced probably saved many lives.

During her second year as senator, Martha was pregnant with her third child. She was also chairing the Public Health Committee. That year, she sponsored Senate Bill 40, which set up greater protections against infectious diseases, and Senate Bill 1, which authorized construction of a hospital for the Utah State School for the Deaf and Dumb. She tried but failed to pass a bill to mandate teaching the harmful effects of drugs and alcohol to schoolchildren.

When her two-session term was up, Cannon did not run again. Governor Heber Wells had appointed her to serve on the State Board of Health. She worked for the welfare of the state from that position and started a medical practice of her own.

During its centennial celebration in 1996, the state honored Martha Cannon's accomplishments with a statue in the Utah State Capitol. Utah did not elect another woman state senator until twenty-three years later. Today, Utah women remain a visible minority on Capitol Hill.

JESSE KNIGHT DREAMS UP
THE HUMBUG MINE

- 1896 -

JESSE KNIGHT HAD BEEN POOR FOR MUCH OF HIS LIFE and had often dreamed of striking it rich. Jesse's mother was a widow who had brought her seven children across the plains from Nauvoo, Illinois, in the 1847 Mormon exodus to Utah. His small ranch in Payson was all Jesse could show for a lifetime of work.

Jesse frequently had visits from miners working in nearby Eureka. They told him stories of rich deposits of ore. Jesse studied the mines, and he soon learned to look for the lime-colored rock that held precious gold, silver, and lead. Whenever he and his sons herded cattle in the area around his ranch, Jesse searched the ground for gold.

One day, Jesse was particularly depressed. He had learned that a man he thought was his friend was planning to cheat him in business. He left his boys at the ranch and went off by himself to the east side of Godiva Mountain, a short distance east of Eureka. As he contemplated his troubles under the boughs of a pine tree, Jesse heard a voice telling him that the country there was for Mormons. Jesse wasn't dreaming; he was wide awake.

The land around Godiva Mountain had belonged to Chief Tintic's people. Mormon pioneers had later settled it, and prospectors had discovered gold in the area. However, the part of the mountain Jesse sat on was the wrong kind of limestone to contain precious metal. Still, the words Jesse heard gave him a strong feeling that he should dig right there.

Jesse trusted his feeling. He lived in a world that was both practical and spiritual. Because of his low regard for Mormon authorities, he had spent the first part of his adult life believing in no church. He grew up championing the underdog, and in Utah, he viewed non-Mormons as underdogs. He felt that, as a minority, non-Mormons were unfairly treated.

Lately, Jesse had undergone a religious transformation. A rat had poisoned his well, and his whole family had fallen ill with a fever. The youngest child, Jennie, was near dying. Jesse's wife, a devout Mormon, implored him to allow the Mormon elders to come and pray over Jennie. He resisted, but finally gave in. After the blessing, Jennie recovered. Soon, though, the oldest of his five children, Minnie, became gravely ill. She told her father of a promise she had made to God: she had asked God to take her life in exchange for Jennie's. She told him she would live for only thirty more days. Minnie died a month later.

Jesse felt intense pain and remorse. He remembered that when Minnie was young, she had almost died of diphtheria. He had promised God then that he would never forget Him if Minnie lived. Jesse had not kept his promise, and now, Minnie was dead. He prayed for forgiveness and dedicated his life to service.

Perhaps that is why, when Jesse heard the voice so loud and clear, he knew what to do. He staked out a claim on a small mine on

Godiva Mountain. He asked his brother-in-law, Jared Roundy, to go in with him on the mine. Roundy had experience in the district's mines. He thought Jesse was crazy. Under no circumstances, he declared, would he be part of such a humbug. Jesse called his dig the Humbug Mine.

Jesse had no money of his own to invest. He went to a friend, cattle buyer Jim McHatton. Jim helped Jesse at first, but then he had misgivings, so Jesse gave him his money back. Finally, Jesse convinced a bank to loan him money. He hired Thomas Leatham and Thomas Mansfield to help him and his son, William. They built a one-room shack on the mountain and started to dig.

For two months, they worked eight-hour shifts, removing rock from the tunnel with wheelbarrows. On one of their trips up the mountain, Jesse told William they would be rich one day. But first, he said, they needed to learn how to handle being rich. He also predicted they would be able to give large amounts of their earnings to the Mormon Church.

Late one afternoon, Leatham ran up the hill, arriving all out of breath to show Jesse a rock that looked like lead ore. William was so excited, he ran to the mine the next morning. Jesse, who had known this was coming, climbed calmly into the mine, loaded a wheelbarrow with the ore, and pushed it up to the tunnel entrance. Emptying it on the ground, he announced that he would never again do work another man could do. From that point on, he would be providing jobs for others.

The Humbug Mine produced gold, silver, and lead; it was one of the richest lead-silver deposits in the West. Jesse claimed that he was lead by divine inspiration. An assayer who worked with him said Jesse made his money with his fantastic memory, his hands-on experience with ores, and an extra sense that enabled him to know where to dig. Time after time, Jesse would walk into a mine, face a rock wall, point, and tell his miners to go that way. Inevitably, they would find rich ore.

Jesse continued to purchase land adjoining the Humbug Mine. He mined an ore body two miles long worth ten million dollars.

Jesse made an unusual mining magnate, and the mining town he built was unique. He allowed no saloons, bars, or houses of ill repute in Knightsville. Instead, he built sixty-five houses and a church that also served as a meeting hall. He provided dances, parties, theater, and sports programs to keep his workers from frequenting Eureka's dens of iniquity.

The majority of Jesse's workers were Mormon, but he forbade his superintendent from asking them about religion or politics. And though union activity disrupted most of the mines in the region, Jesse had little trouble. He took care of his workers. The wages were higher in Knight's mines than anywhere else. Because he didn't want his men working on Sunday, Jesse paid them more so they didn't have to work the extra day. Jesse didn't force his workers to patronize the company boarding houses as other mines did. No hospital funds or insurance fees were deducted from his workers' wages.

Jesse was ruthless in only one area. He believed that men who drank to excess were neglecting their families, and he wouldn't tolerate it. He fired anyone who was caught drinking. Because of Knight's unusual policies, his mines were dubbed "The Sunday School Mines."

Jesse Knight became a philanthropist. He was a major benefactor of the fledgling Brigham Young University. He created many businesses unrelated to mining, just to give people jobs. He lived what he had come to believe: that he was only a keeper of the Lord's earth, and it was his job to help others with whatever riches he was given.

BUTCH CASSIDY AND THE CASTLE
GATE ROBBERY

- 1897 -

BUTCH CASSIDY HAILED FROM CIRCLEVILLE, UTAH, and few there had anything to say against him. Women and children appreciated his polite manner, and his generosity was legendary. The son of a Jack (non-practicing) Mormon, the outlaw seldom drank in excess. He mostly stayed out of folks' way, a trait greatly appreciated in rural Utah.

Butch Cassidy may have started his outlaw career as a cattle rustler, but few took note. Many central Utah ranchers saw little harm in picking up stray, unbranded calves from the unfenced range and taking them home for branding. Things just worked that way in rural Utah in the late 1800s.

True, Butch was a wanted man. His reputation as a bank and train robber in Wyoming followed him everywhere. But other than a bit of cattle rustling, he had always behaved himself in his home state of Utah.

So, few paid any attention when Cassidy rode into the town of Castle Gate on the outskirts of Price, Utah, in April 1897. No one said a thing about him hanging around the saloon for a week, riding his spirited gray horse to the station to meet every train. Why worry about a pleasant stranger when the coal company made unscheduled payroll deliveries to prevent holdups?

Cassidy was patient and lucky. On one trip to the station, he noticed that certain bags the men heaved from the train were weighing them down quite a bit. Before the men could take the bags up the outside stairs to the Pleasant Valley Coal Company, Butch pulled his gun on them. He told them to put down the sacks and put up their hands. One man resisted and was hit over the head by Butch's sidekick, Elza Lay. Another did as he was told, while the third man dropped his bag and dove into a store downstairs.

Butch picked up two sacks and a satchel, tossing some of the loot to Lay. His horse balked at carrying the heavy bags, but Butch spurred him on. Lay and a third robber followed as he rode away. Outside of town, two back-up gang members joined them.

The robbery had been a cinch. The many witnesses included a hundred men who were waiting in town for their paychecks, but efforts to halt the robbery were halfhearted. Someone fired a few ineffectual shots after them, but no one gave chase. Butch had cut the telegraph lines to the town, so word didn't get to the law until the gang had a good head start. Their plan was impeccable and included a relay point where fresh horses waited to help cover the 60 miles between Price and Robber's Roost, the gang's hideout.

Historians disagree on how the gang actually escaped. Author Charles Kelly believes Butch divided the money among several horsemen going in different directions to confuse pursuers. Historian Pearl Baker claims Butch and his accomplices rode straight south through the canyon country to Robber's Roost.

Robber's Roost was in rugged, remote terrain with box canyons, which are still difficult to explore today. Even when a posse came after them, Butch and his gang were relatively safe. The Roost was a perfect place to avoid lawmen such as Joe Meeks (brother of Butch's gang member, Bob Meeks) who led one posse. Anyone who tried to reach the gang from any direction had to cross deserts that had little water, the Dirty Devil River with its steep canyon walls, or the Henry Mountains, the last range in the United States to be mapped. Parts of the gang's escape route passed over hard sandstone that held no hoof prints.

Other outlaws used Robber's Roost as a hideout, but when Cassidy returned to Utah from Wyoming, he was the undisputed leader of the Roost. With his generosity and good manners, Butch cultivated friends in the territory around the hideout. Stories say he bought dinner from widows using gold pieces. Cassidy bragged that he never robbed people—only banks and railroads—and that he had never shot anyone.

Butch felt it was his duty to keep his gang safe and provided for them. After the Castle Gate holdup, he sent gang members to Price and Green River to buy food and ammunition. Their main supply point, however, was the tiny, dusty little hamlet of Hanksville, in the middle of nowhere. Charley Gibbons ran a store there where Cassidy liked to shop. When Butch was seventeen years old, he had worked for Charley as a cowhand.

Though Robber's Roost was a perfect place to escape the law, it had a fault. The only nightlife it offered were poker games and coyote serenades. In July the gang finally decided to spend their money on fun over the border in Baggs, Wyoming. By the time they were through eating, drinking, and shooting up the place, they had become legends. Folks say they paid the saloon owner for his trouble, and he was able to open a fancy place in Rawlins a short time later.

Being on the run all the time was hard on Cassidy. Some said he never meant to become an outlaw; it wasn't in his nature. After Elza

Lay was wounded and sentenced to prison and Bob Meeks lost his leg trying to escape from prison, Cassidy made an attempt to go straight. He visited a prominent Salt Lake City attorney and tried to work out a deal with Utah Governor Heber Wells. In exchange for clemency, he wanted a real job protecting railroads from being robbed. The deal fell through, and Butch went back to robbing trains.

Legend has it that Butch lost his life in a shootout in South America. He went to Bolivia with the Sundance Kid and Etta Pace, first trying to go straight and eventually robbing more trains. The movie *Butch Cassidy and the Sundance Kid,* starring Paul Newman as Butch and Robert Redford as the Kid, portrays a version of the famous outlaws' final moments.

But many insist that Butch escaped that jam. His friends and family say he survived and returned to the United States, changed his name to William Phillips, married, and worked as a draftsman. They claim he wrote a book of his life called *The Bandit Invincible* and tried to sell it to publishers and a movie company. Eventually, they say, he died of cancer.

While his time as an outlaw in Utah was brief, Cassidy's legend adds a colorful chapter to the state's history. Many in Utah say they saw and talked to him after 1902, but no one ever turned him in. The friendships he had formed kept him free throughout his life.

SCOFIELD'S MINE DISASTER

- 1900 -

Sara Donaldson woke early on Tuesday morning. She had a lot to do to prepare for the evening's May first Dewey Day celebrations (to celebrate Admiral Dewey's defeat of the Spanish at the Battle of Manila in the Philippines). Usually, she would wake up her husband and son so they could eat a hearty breakfast before their shift in the mine. But today, Sara hesitated. A dark feeling came over her and settled in a knot in her stomach. She would let them sleep in today; she would go to the company store for baking supplies before she disturbed them. While Sara was gone, Walt stirred and slowly opened his eyes. The house was quiet. It seemed late. He must have overslept. Where was Sara? She had never let him oversleep before. He woke his son, John, and told him to hurry and get ready for work: they were late. Walt didn't know whether to be nervous or mad.

Shortly after 10 A.M., Walt stepped outside and saw Sara returning. Before they could speak, a low boom—like thunder—rolled across the valley. The sound came from deep in the mountain, breaking the morning's calm. Many people in Scofield first thought it was a salute for Dewey Day. Then they saw the billowing black clouds and smelled the acrid smoke pouring from the Number Four mine. Their hearts sank as the truth registered.

Coal miners everywhere live in fear of an explosion. But in Scofield, the Winter Quarters Mine had recently been inspected and declared one of the nation's safest. The mine's owners, the Pleasant Valley Coal Company, contracted with the Navy to supply two thousand tons of coal a day. Three hundred miners worked hard to fill that order. It was the first of the month, and each miner had carried a twenty-five-pound keg of black powder with him into the mine to blast out his portion of the bituminous coal seam. The miners were paid sixty-five cents for each ton of coal they hauled out, so many men took young sons with them to help fill their cars. Occasionally, a wife followed her husband to work.

Walt hugged Sara and ran with John to do what they could at the mine. What they saw would haunt them forever. They were the fortunate survivors but the unfortunate witnesses of the worst mining disaster America had ever seen.

No one could say how many people were in the mine that day, but by 10 A.M., most miners were at their stations. A flame from a miner's carbide lamp probably sparked the explosion by igniting coal dust in the air. The tunnel floors were usually sprinkled with water to keep the dust down, but the precaution hadn't worked. In a chain reaction, the powder kegs ignited, and the fireball ripped through the tunnel of Number Four.

As the force of the blast burst from the mine entrance, it threw miner John Wilson two hundred yards across the gully in a shower of splintered timbers and twisted metal. His friends tenderly picked him up, gingerly holding his crushed skull, and lifting his body off a stake protruding from his abdomen. Amazingly, he survived.

Inside Number Four, rescue workers led by mine superintendent Thomas J. Parmley found smoke, debris, and dead horses blocking the way. To save time, they rushed to Number One, which was connected to Number Four. Will Clark ran ahead; his father and brother were inside. The rescue party called after him. They remembered another danger: afterdamp. As an explosion eats up oxygen in a mine, an invisible mixture of carbon dioxide, carbon monoxide, nitrogen, and other gasses takes its place. The silent killer claimed Will. The rescue party was forced back to Number Four until they could get oxygen into Number One.

As workers cleared the entrance to Number Four, air entered the tunnel. The men began removing the burned and mangled bodies in coal cars, while distraught mothers, wives, and children moaned and wailed. The clerk at the Wasatch Store knew every man from the mine. Today, his job was to identify and tag each body as it came into the makeshift morgue set up in Edward's boarding house. The pile of boots and clothes outside the building grew higher as the day progressed. When the boarding house was full, they carted the bodies to the school.

Later, rescue workers found more dead miners in Number One. They had fallen when the gas reached them, with a sandwich, pipe, or tool in hand. One young man had fallen with his arms around another's waist, overcome in the act of helping his companion to safety.

Some survived. Fifteen-year-old Tom Pugh clamped his hat between his teeth and over his nose and ran a mile and a half through the dark to safety. James Naylor tried to close the door of Number Six just as it and he were blown into the air. Naylor landed two cars away in a tunnel ditch, then found his way out. After the blast threw them 300 feet, Ephraim Rowe helped Sam Wycherly crawl 1,200 feet to the entrance. One hundred and three men were lucky that day, but only one man walked out of Number Four alive. Those who waited too long or ran the wrong way into the afterdamp died.

Rescuers came from nearby mines to help. Grim-faced, they worked into the night. They removed body after body, hoping to find someone alive. Local miners such as Walt Donaldson had the hardest time. Every dead face he saw belonged to a neighbor or a friend. To keep from breaking down and becoming useless, the miners ceased to feel or to think; they could only act.

As news of the explosion reached the outside world, help flowed in. Flowers, food, money, and coffins came from Salt Lake City and throughout the state. The coal company donated burial clothes, caskets, and money to the victims' families.

On Saturday, a Lutheran minister presided over a funeral for sixty-one Finnish miners at Scofield Cemetery. The Mormons held their service later. Two funeral trains transported families and caskets to cities all over Utah. In Salt Lake City, the Catholic Knights of Columbus met the train to help bury three Italians.

Some of the dead remained in the caved-in tunnels of Winter Quarters Mine. The Finnish miners were sure several of their countrymen were inside, undiscovered and unknown since many Finnish immigrants were single men who did not speak English and had no relatives or friends to notice they were gone.

The official number of fatalities was 200, yet the unofficial estimate was set at 246. The grief of the 107 widows and 268 orphans is incomprehensible; the litany of tragedy is exhausting. Every home was affected. Abe Louma and his wife had come from Finland to join seven sons and three grandsons who worked in the mine. All of the men, except one son, were lost. The Hunter family lost ten members. Passengers in the funeral train tried in vain to console a hysterical young woman as the caskets of her father, her two brothers, and her husband of three months were transferred to a train bound for Richfield.

Catholic Bishop Lawrence Scanlan opened the doors of St. Ann's Orphanage in Salt Lake City to the orphans and the children of women who needed time to recover their lives. Women volunteered to come to Scofield to cook and help the widows. Sara did what she could to help. She didn't have much time to contemplate the premonition she had had on the morning of the disaster. After living through the horror of that day, the survivors still had a big question to consider: "Can we go into the mines again?"

An inquiry determined that the Pleasant Valley Coal Company was not at fault in the explosion. The company voluntarily instituted more safety measures. One by one, men decided whether or not to go back to work. Like miners all over the world, most went back to their livelihood, praying that nothing like the tragedy of May 1, 1900, would ever happen again.

WOMEN OF KANAB MAKE HISTORY

- 1912 -

ON NOVEMBER 7, 1912, THE SMALL SOUTHEASTERN Utah town of Kanab held one of the strangest elections in the state's history. No one could say how it started; likely, it began with a typical conversation about local politics.

Everyone knew each other in Kanab, and everyone had an opinion about how the town was run. Someone probably complained about the town council. Maybe the councilmen spent more time out of town on cattle and sheep business than they did taking care of Kanab's needs. The women, especially, were always finding fault with the council. But no one had a solution; at least no one had bothered to run for council or even for mayor, so an election wouldn't help.

Then, as a dare or a joke, someone submitted a list of names to put on the ballot for the town's elected positions. No one told the candidates of their nominations. Each name was a woman's; they all ran unopposed, and they all won. Mary Elizabeth Wooley Chamberlain, the new mayor of Kanab, became the second woman mayor in the

United States. The Kanab town council became the first all-woman council in the country. Without making a single formal speech, the women of Kanab ended up in charge and became instant celebrities.

The Utah state constitution had given women the vote in 1896, but not until 1920 would the Nineteenth Amendment to the U.S. Constitution grant all women the right to vote. The election of an all-female town council was unheard of. Newspapers from all over the country and the world called to get the story. Susa Young Gates, a noted suffragist, visited the newly elected women and offered her support.

At first, Mary Chamberlain and her friends dismissed the whole thing as a mistake. Most people in town knew little about what the town council really did, and few could even name the council members. But everyone knew Mary. When she was twenty-six and single, she had been elected county clerk for Kanab—she was the first Utah woman to hold such a position. Mary also helped out regularly at the general store. Through her kind dealings with neighbors, she had developed a good reputation.

Instead of laughing, the town citizens and the elected women's families threw their support behind the mayor and her council. The editor of the local newspaper, D. D. Rust, wrote a complimentary story about them. The women themselves discussed and debated whether or not to accept the positions. Finally, they decided they couldn't do any worse than past councilmen. They would answer the challenge and do their best.

The old council members held more meetings than usual at the end of their term: four in December and one more in January. Mary felt the men were worried about the women taking over and wanted to tidy up the town business before they left.

Vinnie Jepson, though honored, gave up her seat to Ada Pratt Seegmiller, who joined Luella Atkin McAllister, Blanche Robinson

Hamblin, Tamar Stewart Hamblin, and Mary Elizabeth Wooley Chamberlain in governing Kanab. The women held only their first and last council meetings in the courthouse. For the next two years, they met at members' homes, feeling the courthouse was "too masculine."

The council immediately took a close look at Kanab and began working diligently to make it a better place to live. Its agenda gives a glimpse into small town life of the period. Early on, the women passed a resolution to keep cattle off the sidewalks and streets; and horses were not to be tied on the sidewalks. They imposed fines on anyone who let waste water run down the streets, anyone who allowed cattle or horses to run loose in the streets, and any boy or girl who shot a slingshot at a bird in town.

One of the council's first concerns was to protect local merchants. They increased the cost of the license a traveling salesman had to buy in order to sell goods in Kanab. They ordered construction of a dike to prevent flooding. They had the cemetery surveyed and began charging fees for plots. And they charged the board of health with inspecting all pigpens, stockyards, stables, and corrals in town for cleanliness.

The women shouldered the responsibility for protecting Kanab's morals as well. Because Mormons hold that Sunday is a day for church and rest, the council ordered stores not to sell unnecessary articles on Sunday. They prohibited horse races and ball games on the Sabbath, and outlawed gambling and games of chance at any time.

Many towns in Utah were dry, and the town council made sure that Kanab discouraged the selling of liquor. The mayor authorized searches for illegal alcohol. On one occasion, the sheriff seized twelve gallons of whiskey; the council ordered six poured out, and the remaining six saved for medicinal purposes. The council's complaint to the Post Office that mail carriers were transporting liquor from Marysville to Kanab ended the practice.

The women didn't neglect to beautify their city. They declared September 12, 1912, as "stinkweed day" and offered prizes to citizens who rid their yards and sidewalks of the weed. Most blocks in Kanab had only four houses with large yards and lots of sidewalk, so homeowners had to labor hard for a reward.

Though town council membership and the work they did marked the councilwomen as liberated, they insisted they were managing to remain feminine. Every one of the women had between two and seven children, and three of them had babies while in office. Only once did child care become a problem: when one of the husbands was called away in an emergency to shoe a horse, he left the six-month-old with its busy mother.

Mary bragged that she could do it all: take care of her two boys and city business; make quilts, carpets, and soap; and can fruit and vegetables. She also held positions within the Mormon Church and clerked at Bowman's general store.

At the end of their term, the women declined to run again. They encouraged other women to enter city government, but none did. The men took over and things went back to "normal." Many townspeople told Mary that the women's town council accomplished more than the men's ever had. Mary admitted that at times, the councilwomen put up with opposition, even at home. But they had the strength of character to hold their own. And they had the right, next time the town council wasn't doing its job, to complain even louder.

THE TRIAL OF JOE HILL

- 1915 -

READ ALL ABOUT IT! Two men rob a grocery store, fatally shooting the owner and his son. The murderers get away. The authorities round up suspects. The Salt Lake City newspapers published such crime stories every day.

But this time the story was different. One of the suspects in this case was Joe Hill, a well-known labor organizer. When Joe Hill pleaded not guilty as charged on January 22, 1915, he had no idea what he was up against. His trial for burglary and murder was to become a flash point in the struggle between the working class and big business.

Hill had spent the previous five years fighting America's economic system, but he had found little cause to question its judicial system. When he was arrested for murder in Salt Lake City, Hill's fight for the working class became a fight for his life. He claimed he could prove his innocence. To this day, people wonder if he was given a fair chance to do so.

Joe Hill was known for the songs he wrote. He published them for his union, the Industrial Workers of the World (IWW), in the

Little Red Songbook. Organizers used Joe's ditties to motivate and agitate picketers and strikers across the country. Traveling to Utah to work in Park City's Silver King mines, Hill arrived at the moment when Utah miners began to demand better wages and working conditions. Some believed he had come to Park City for more than just a mining job.

With the help of Governor William Spry, the Utah Copper Company had put down one miners' strike. In the next major labor strike, unions had forced the Utah Construction Company to make concessions to its workers. The concessions increased big business's dislike of and powerful opposition to unions.

Unaware that his trial had anything to do with his union activities, Hill acted as his own attorney at his arraignment and preliminary hearing. After the hearing, E. D. McDougall and F. B. Scott offered to defend Hill for free.

As it turned out, the trial delved further into Hill's involvement with the union than into the crime itself. Hill was originally only one of several suspects. The police had arrested Hill because he had been shot the night of the murders—January 10, 1915. After the authorities discovered Joe's ties to the labor unions, he became the only suspect.

The powerful anti-unionists hoped to hurt the unions by attacking their organizers. The judge in Hill's case, M. L. Ritchie, showed an anti-union bias throughout the trial. The prosecuting attorney, E. O. Leatherwood, built the entire case on circumstantial evidence. He characterized Hill as a murderer and an anarchist, condemning him on both points equally.

The only witness to the grocery store killing was thirteen-year-old Merlin Morrison, whose father and brother had died. He testified that two masked men came into his father's grocery store in Salt Lake City at closing time. When his father stood up from behind the counter, the men shouted, "We've got you now!" and shot Mr. Morrison. Merlin was hiding at the back of the store. The boy thought his brother Arling must have grabbed his father's handgun and fired at the murderers. The masked men shot back, killing Arling. Merlin couldn't positively identify Joe Hill, but said he resembled the taller of the two masked men.

Two of Morrison's neighbors saw the masked men run out of the store. Vera Hansen thought she heard one call out to the other that he had been shot. Neither of the two witnesses were sure they had seen Hill, but they agreed that Hill's build was the same as the wounded man's.

The star witness for the prosecution was Dr. Frank McHugh. McHugh had examined Joe Hill in his office at about 11:30 P.M. that night. He said he treated Hill for a bullet that had gone through his chest. A friend, Dr. A. A. Bird, had come by as McHugh was treating Hill. Both saw a gun in a holster fall out of Hill's coat. Hill told them he had been shot in a fight over a woman. Because they did not know of the murders, and because Hill had managed to walk to his office (which was more than 3 miles from Morrison's store) to be treated, McHugh discharged Hill, and Bird drove him to a Swedish friend's boarding house to recuperate. Bird testified that Hill threw a gun out the window of his vehicle on the way.

When he learned of the Morrison murders, McHugh called the police about Hill.

The next witness, Phoebe Seeley, was walking in front of the store when the masked men ran past her. She testified that the taller man had facial features like Hill's, including a scar on his neck. But she couldn't positively identify Hill either.

Leatherwood had other "proof" of Hill's guilt. Police had searched Hill's room and found a red bandanna matching the description of the handkerchiefs worn by the murderers. The prosecution claimed that blood on the pavement outside the store proved Arling had wounded his attackers. In addition, a record of Hill's purchase of a gun in Salt Lake City was entered as evidence.

The defense maintained Hill's innocence. It argued that Merlin did not see Arling shoot the intruder. A complete search of the store had turned up no bullets from Arling's gun. Dr. McHugh said the bullet had exited Hill's body; where was the bullet? Hill's attorney tried to put a firearms expert on the stand to show that the lead bullet from Morrison's gun would not have made the kind of wound Hill suffered. Judge Ritchie would not allow the witness to testify.

Ritchie suppressed much of the evidence in Hill's favor. M. F. Beer wanted to testify that holes in Hill's coat were lower than his wounds, and that, therefore, he must have had his hands up when he was shot. A person in the act of shooting would have his hands at shoulder level or below. The judge refused to allow Dr. Beer's testimony. The defense called a gun shop salesclerk to the stand. Hill had purchased a gun on the day of the murder, and the clerk could testify that he sold Hill a Luger. Morrison was shot with a Colt automatic. The clerk's statement was also suppressed.

The judge also refused to share a few salient details with the jury. No one had proven that the blood outside the store was human blood. And the red bandanna in Hill's possession was given to him after the murders by his Swedish friend who ran the boarding house.

Ritchie also withheld from the jury the information that other suspects had been arrested for the murders and then released. Jurors didn't hear that Morrison had twice before shot at intruders, wounding them. They also didn't know that Morrison had suspected two of his neighbors of wanting to kill him. He had specifically told his wife that should he be killed, the police should question certain people who he named. Ritchie didn't reveal that Morrison was a former policeman and that he feared someone he had once arrested would come back for revenge. Or that one of these men, Frank Z. Wilson, had just been released from prison and was picked up in the vicinity the night of the murders.

Though it came out that no robbery was ever attempted, prosecutors never bothered to establish another motive for Hill to commit the murder.

Ritchie told Hill he could only clear himself by revealing the name of the woman whose honor he claimed he had been protecting. Hill refused.

Midway through the trial, Hill fired his attorneys. He believed they were not being forceful enough in their questioning of witnesses who had changed their testimony between his hearing and his trial. He told the judge he wanted to question the witnesses himself. Instead of excusing the jury while Hill complained and allowing Hill to find another lawyer, Judge Ritchie let the trial continue, and the lawyers questioned witnesses as friends of the court. This did not help Hill.

Too late, Hill's friends managed to engage two more powerful attorneys, Judge Orrin Nelson Hilton and Soren X. Christensen, to represent Hill. Joe Hill was found guilty and sentenced to death.

The governor of Utah, the Utah Supreme Court, and the Board of Pardons received hundreds of letters of protest and thousands of signatures on petitions. The unions gave Hill's defense team money and enlisted outside help. The Swedish Minister to the United States (Joe was Swedish) and President Woodrow Wilson personally requested a pardon or a new trial. The Utah authorities remained firm, insisting that Hill had received a fair trial. They resented outsiders telling them they had done a bad job.

During his incarceration, Joe continued to write songs and organize from his jail cell. He told his fellow labor leaders not to mourn for him, but to continue his work for the unions. Joe Hill was executed at the Utah State Penitentiary (the present site of Sugar House Park) on November 19, 1915. He fought until the end, then he himself gave the firing squad the order to fire.

UTAH GETS A BAD CASE OF THE FLU

- 1918 -

DORA PETERSON'S BROTHER, ANGUS, FELT TERRIBLE. He burned with fever. His eyes hurt. His chest hurt. His head hurt. The flu he'd caught was a bad one. Then, on December 20, 1918, Angus died. Dora was baffled—how could he have been so healthy and full of life one day and gone the next?

The awful thing about this flu was that it killed indiscriminately— young, old, weak, or healthy; it didn't matter to the flu. Since October, all of Utah had been battling the Spanish Flu.

Dora did what she could to help Angus's widow, Polly. Polly was sick with both grief and the flu. Dora took care of Polly and Angus's five children, who ranged in age from eighteen months to eight years. She talked with the bishop and planned a small funeral service for Angus at Polly's home.

Riverton, Utah, like most other Utah towns, was under quarantine. Citizens could not meet in groups anywhere—not for a funeral, for church, or for school. Whenever Dora left the house, she had to wear a gauze mask. Dora's son Joe had an evening paper route. His customers feared he might carry the infection from home to home, so they put the money they owed him in an envelope or a handkerchief in the mailbox.

Polly died just before Christmas. Dora didn't know what to do. She took the children home with her and quarantined them in the front room. For ten days, Dora and her family delivered food to the children, placing the meals slightly inside the door to their room. The eight-year-old fed the baby, and the others did the best they could. Dora's grief at losing Angus and Polly and her pain in not being able to comfort their children were tempered by the fear of what the flu could do to her own family. All over the state, families struggled with similar dilemmas.

The Spanish Flu was so named because eight million people in Spain contracted the disease, but the epidemic may have originated at Fort Riley, Kansas. American troops were training there for entry into World War I. More than 1,100 men at Fort Riley got sick, and 46 died after inhaling smoke from burning manure. Men from the Fort went to Europe, taking the disease with them. Half of the soldiers who died in Europe were killed by the virus rather than bullets. From Europe, the flu spread to China, Africa, Brazil, and the South Pacific. It killed 21 million people in four months.

American soldiers coming home from the war brought the flu back with them. A soldier in Coalville, Utah, got a haircut; the next day, everyone in the shop was sick. The disease spread. In the end, about 675,000 Americans died of Spanish Flu, about ten times more than the number of American soldiers who died in action during World War I.

Most people stayed home. It seemed the best way to avoid contagion. The Health Department said the disease was spread and caught through the respiratory system and that there was no cure.

The inoculations they had tried didn't work. The only thing victims could do, they said, was to stay in bed, keep a healthy diet, and get help from a doctor. The most common doctor's prescription was whiskey. In Utah, purchasing alcohol was illegal, and the nation was in the process of passing the Eighteenth Amendment instituting prohibition. Still, doctors could prescribe alcohol for medicinal purposes. Whiskey couldn't have done much for the patients except ease their suffering, but most of them took it anyway.

Larger cities enacted strict laws to keep the flu from spreading. They turned schools into hospitals; they quarantined or excluded newcomers. The November elections were held outside in tents. In smaller towns, neighbors helped each other out. Those who were healthy milked neighbors' cows and brought food to their ill friends.

Towns appeared to be deserted. Signs lettered with the word INFLUENZA hung on doors. Shopkeepers wore masks. Any business where people worked together was hit hard. The epidemic crippled mines and factories. In some school districts, 90 percent of the children contracted the flu. Teachers from the closed schools volunteered for the Red Cross.

Just as the big cities began to bring the epidemic under control, World War I ended. On November 11, 1918, hundreds of people spontaneously poured into the streets, shouting and making noise with whatever objects they could lay their hands on. Afterward, the flu spread fast. In the next four days, Ogden reported 357 new cases. It was the same everywhere.

In January, the 145th Light Artillery Field Regiment came back from France to Ogden as heroes. The community debated whether it would be safe to welcome them with a parade. City officials decided to cancel the celebrations, but the army assured them that none of the men were sick. The city modified the parade plans in order to limit personal contact, but the precaution proved impossible to enforce. The people were jubilant; they discarded their masks and the toll rose even higher.

Slowly, the epidemic wore itself out. The Utah State Health Department estimated that in two years, the Spanish Flu had infected 91,799 people and killed 2,915. Utah, Colorado, and Pennsylvania were the hardest hit states in the union. Utahns' large families contributed to the high toll.

The people who suffered most in Utah, however, were the Indians. The disease wiped out whole communities of Native Americans. The Navajo, Ute, and Paiute lived in remote areas with no health care except their medicine men. Navajo healing ceremonies, while they helped the patient, were performed in close quarters and allowed the disease to spread. Tradition dictated that when a person died, his house must be burned to enable his spirit to leave. In most cases, houses were simply abandoned. The rest of the family, left homeless, were even more vulnerable to the illness.

Marie Lehi, a Paiute, lost her brother and his wife. She told of entering a community where everyone was dead except a baby. The Paiute population was decimated. Surviving Paiutes became a minority in the Indian community, and the Navajo took over much of their land.

The Navajo said they had seen the epidemic coming. A solar eclipse in June of 1918 had been a warning. Sunsets that summer and fall had been particularly red and ominous. A tree disease that turned the tips of pinyon and juniper branches brown also foretold a sickness that would reach humans.

The eventual epidemic not only caused a great many deaths, it had a tragic affect on almost every family in Utah.

CHARLIE GLASS AND THE SHEEP
AND CATTLE WAR

- 1921 -

CHARLIE GLASS, FOREMAN for the Lazy Y Cross cattle ranch, was mad. He saw a herd of sheep greedily munching grass down to its roots just a mile inside the Lazy Y property line. Glass's boss, Oscar L. Turner, needed that grass to keep his smaller, weaker calves alive. Charlie knew he had to do something.

In February 1921 sheep and cattle ranchers in southeastern Utah had called a shaky truce in their range war. They agreed to set aside part of the public rangeland for cattle and part for sheep. The quarantine line was supposed to protect the cattle from sheep diseases and prevent cattlemen and sheepmen from fighting. But the Basque sheepmen kept breaking their word. Charlie was tired of catching the sheepmen and their herds trespassing on territory marked specifically for cattle by sheep inspector H. E. Herbert.

Just four days earlier, Charlie and a fellow cowpuncher, Jimmy Warner, had argued with some sheepherders hired by William

Fitzpatrick. One herder, Gerrold Yaber, had threatened to cut the bridle reins on Jimmy's horse. Jimmy pulled out his gun. Gerrold ran to his tent to get his gun, but Charlie got there first and hid it. When the sheepherder failed to find his gun, the two cattle ranchers suggested they have a nice talk; they managed to convince Gerrold to move his sheep.

Charlie took pride in protecting his boss's range from the sheep ranchers. He used his large build and larger horse to intimidate the Basque sheepherders. What's more, Glass hadn't done anything to discourage rumors that the gun he carried underneath his coat had notches in it numbering the men he had killed in Indian territory.

But Glass's methods didn't seem to be working. The sheepherders, openly belligerent, were encroaching again. Charlie tried to remain calm as he approached the Basques, but he remembered what had happened four days earlier. While his partner circled from behind, Charlie dismounted and went to talk to another of William Fitzpatrick's sheepherders, Felix Jesui. Charlie asked Felix to move his sheep. Felix refused. Charlie threatened to talk to his boss, Oscar Turner. Turner would show Felix himself what he felt about sheep trespassing on his land. Charlie turned to leave. As he reached his horse, bullets whizzed past his head. Charlie turned and fired back. Felix fell dead.

Charlie mounted his horse. He rode to the ranch to tell Turner what had happened and turn himself in to the sheriff. His partner disappeared.

As Charlie faced the sheriff, he must have felt a pang of apprehension. He was a black man, and he knew that justice was not the same for someone of his race, especially in small, rural towns where few Blacks lived. Yet Charlie trusted his community. He had worked on Turner's ranch for four years, giving orders to white cowhands. He had earned a reputation as a good cowboy, especially in the bronc riding department. Charlie also liked to drink and play poker with friends. Everyone but the sheepmen treated him with respect.

Turner came to the aid of his foreman and friend. He posted Charlie's bond of $10,000 and hired a defense lawyer, hoping to prove that no one should mess with a cattleman. Glass appreciated the help. In return, he deeded the homestead he owned on the outskirts of Turner's ranch to his boss.

Glass's supporters worried that he wouldn't get a fair trial in a town where the cattle-sheep war raged. After considerable debate, the authorities set Glass's trial for November 1921 in Moab. At the time, Moab was a small ranching community surrounded by majestic red cliffs and flanked by the chocolate-colored Colorado River.

On the day of the trial, the courtroom was packed. Charlie was a popular man, and many had taken sides. A reporter from the *Moab Times-Independent* documented the trial, which made front page news.

As the trial opened, Basque sheepherder Eusebis Astegarga described how he worked with Felix Jesui and others herding sheep for William Fitzpatrick. He detailed the conflicts between the Turner cattlemen and Fitzpatrick's sheepmen in the days before the murder. He had heard shots that day, but he didn't investigate. A fellow sheepherder had told him of Jesui's death. That herder was with cattleman Oscar Turner when Glass came to report the shooting. Turner sent the sheepherder to stay with the body and went with Glass to see the sheriff.

The doctor who examined Felix said the sheepman was killed by a bullet to the right temple. He said he also found bullet shells about 20 feet away from Felix, where Glass allegedly stood as Felix fired at him.

The sheriff testified that Felix had two guns on him, a rifle and an automatic pistol. He agreed with the doctor. He too had seen footprints and bullet casings from Felix's gun where Glass said he was standing, proving that Felix had shot at Charlie.

The jury heard testimony from two sheepherders describing past conflicts with the cattlemen. Then sheep inspector H. E. Herbert told of problems he had had with Fitzpatrick's sheepmen. They had bragged to him that they would graze their sheep where they wanted. They had threatened to come back next year and graze their sheep until the grass was gone. Herbert, too, had felt threatened by the armed sheepherders. The inspector said he had warned them to stay within the quarantine lines and to stop using intimidating tactics.

After Glass testified, telling his side of the story, the jury retired to make their decision. They deliberated for two hours. At midnight, they declared Glass not guilty. No riots met the verdict. In fact, Glass became a hero of sorts. But he was wary after the trial and carried his gun everywhere. He never knew when a vindictive sheepherder might seek revenge.

As the years passed, many forgot the incident. Charlie continued to work for Turner, won money here and there in rodeos and poker games, and occasionally enjoyed a good drink.

Every so often, Charlie traveled into the tiny hamlet of Thompson (now called Thompson Springs), near Moab, to play poker, sometimes with friends and relatives of Felix, the man he had killed. After sixteen years, he must have decided they were his friends too. One night, Glass ended up in the back of a pickup truck bound for Thompson with some sheepherders. Later, some of Glass's friends said he trusted the herders. Others said he would never have gotten into the truck if he hadn't been drinking. A few speculated that he had been knocked on the head and carried to the back of the truck.

The only known facts are that the pickup rolled off the road that night and Glass died of a broken neck. The sheepherders emerged unscathed. Some believed it was an accident; others remained convinced that the sheepherders had only made it look that way and that they were not even in the truck when it rolled off the road.

The town where Glass was buried overlooked its practice of banning Negroes in the cemetery. Charlie Glass was buried in a Fruita, Colorado, graveyard, near members of the Turner family.

CHIEF POSEY AND
THE LAST INDIAN WAR

- 1923 -

As Chief Posey lay alone on the sandstone ledge, dying from a bullet wound in his hip, help was as near as the lights from the town of Blanding, which twinkled below him. But he didn't move. He stuffed herbs and grass into the wound, but the poison was already in his blood. It would destroy this man as inevitably as the coming of the settlers had obliterated his people's way of life.

After Chief Posey's death, people asked, "Why didn't he save himself? Did he not trust even his own tribe to help him? Was he tired of fighting? Or did he think he could win this last battle alone?" Perhaps his story will offer some answers.

Chief Posey, known as a leader of a small band of Paiutes, grew up in the Four Corners region, near Navajo Mountain and what is now Rainbow Bridge National Monument. His people, the Paiutes, had been nomads. Family groups had hunted, gathered, and lived together. They had coexisted and even intermarried with another nomadic tribe, the Utes. But as Posey reached adulthood, the Indians' lives began to change.

In 1879 Mormon pioneers settled in southeastern Utah. The Mormons needed the valleys for farms and the mountains for grazing cattle and sheep in the summer. Eventually, the settlers displaced Chief Posey's people. For a while, the Chief and his band coexisted in relative peace with the Mormon settlers. The Paiutes often came into town or onto a ranch to ask for a hand out such as flour or melons. Brigham Young had instructed the settlers to share what they could: it was easier to feed the Paiutes than fight them. The occasional pony or steer appropriated by the local Indians angered the settlers, but they knew they were outnumbered; usually, they didn't fight back. Such incidents were viewed as the price of living on land that once belonged to the Indians.

Yet it wasn't long before the settlers' attitude changed. Pressure from miners, cattlemen, and sheep ranchers had forced the Colorado Utes onto the Consolidated Ute Reservation in Utah. The whites considered Paiutes and Utes to be the same, despite their unrelated cultures; the settlers expected the Paiutes to move to the reservation too. Many did, but others refused. Following in his father's nomadic tradition, Posey resisted the reservation life.

At the time, the United States government held a view similar to Posey's: Indians did not remain self-sufficient on the reservations. In 1885 and 1887, Congress passed laws allowing Indians to homestead land on or off the reservation. Many of Chief Posey's people took up the offer. If they homesteaded for twenty-five years, the government promised to grant them United States citizenship.

Unfortunately, the Paiute reservation and its surrounding homesteads lay in the way of big business. Large cattle companies started driving cattle through the Indian lands. The cattle herds caused problems crossing the reservation lands. The huge herds overgrazed the lands used by big game, such as elk, driving the game away. The over-grazing also caused erosion. In the arid climate, eroded soil quickly entered and polluted streams, making them uninhabitable for fish. The Paiutes traditional food sources were disappearing. To survive, they had to find other food.

Since the cattlemen were trespassing on their land, the Indians felt they could take an occasional steer or lamb as payment owed them. But cattle rustlers were operating at the same time, and they stole stock in large numbers. Cattlemen mistakenly blamed many of the thefts on the Indians. To cut their losses, and to get more grazing land for their herds, the cattle companies started a campaign to take the Indians' land for themselves.

During the squabbling, Chief Posey became known as a renegade. He had a penchant for stealing horses and stirring up trouble. He symbolized the Indian's refusal to submit to the white law.

Posey's latest scrape with the law involved the arrest of the sons of his two friends, Joe Bishop and Sanup. The sheriff claimed that the two boys, along with a third boy (the son of Dutchy), had robbed a sheepherder's camp, killed a calf, and burned a bridge. Dutchy's boy died of pneumonia before he could be arrested, but the sheriff took the other two boys into custody.

The boys were held in deputy sheriff John Rogers' house. The sight of their boys surrounded by so many armed guards upset Joe Bishop and Sanup. They asked if they could spend the night to make sure their sons were safe. When the guards left their guns inside and went out to get firewood, no one attempted to escape.

During the night, Joe Bishop's boy fell deathly ill. He blamed his sickness on his dinner of potatoes. Though Deputy Sheriff Rogers suspected a lie, he let the boys go home after they promised to return the next day for their trial.

The next morning, the ill boy's brother came back to complain about the deputy sheriff's wife's cooking. He said his brother had shaken all night "like a poisoned coyote." Though he was weak, Bishop's boy returned with his friend as they had promised. The trial, held in the school basement, was short. The judge found them guilty but did not sentence them immediately. Most thought they would probably spend a short time in jail.

As the boys came out of the school, Chief Posey rode up to rescue them. In a few seconds, the boys escaped, taking Sheriff William Oliver's gun. Someone shot the sheriff's horse. The resulting ruckus gave the authorities an excuse to round up and arrest the forty or so remaining free Paiutes in the area who had no idea what they had done wrong. The sheriff organized a posse, claiming that Posey, as a Paiute leader, might stir up all the Paiutes. The white authorities knew but ignored the fact that most Paiutes did not follow Posey's leadership.

Chief Posey and his small band hid in a maze of sandstone canyons in Cottonwood Wash. The sheriff and his men took up positions around the wash. Reinforcements were ferried from town in a Model T Ford and a Dodge. Sheriff Oliver gave the excited posse orders to shoot.

Posey took up a defensive position in a canyon. His 30.06 rifle outpowered most of the posse's weapons, and he thought he could wait them out. On a run past the posse, he shot the tires and seat of one of the cars. His bullet went through the seat, stopping before it hit the men sitting there. One man thought he had shot Posey, but Posey disappeared. The posse decided to spend the night in Blanding.

A small group of posse members spotted Chief Posey the next day near Comb Reef. He had been to Blanding to see the Paiutes in custody there and was headed for a wisp of smoke near Comb Ridge that he thought signaled the remnants of his band. Posey galloped past the posse members, hanging down on the side of his mare for protection and shooting from under her neck. The posse got off several shots. They figured one of their bullets may have hit him in the hip.

Another posse member, Bill Young, heard the commotion. As he rode down a ridge toward the shooting, he spotted Joe Bishop's boy and Sanup's boy riding toward him up the hill. Young dismounted and hid behind a juniper tree, afraid for his life. He watched as the boys stood in their stirrups; they'd seen his horse and were searching the sagebrush for him. Young shot at Bishop's boy's shirt button and hit his mark, killing the boy. He knew he could hit Sanup's boy too, but he didn't shoot and the boy took off. The two boys had been Bill's friends, and he had already shot one of them.

Neither side knew that Chief Posey was in trouble. For two freezing days and nights, Posey's band waited for him. Finally, they walked into the posse's camp and surrendered. The posse didn't have enough trucks to get them all back to Blanding, so some had to walk part of the way.

The night of the surrender, the townspeople held a mass meeting and decided to fight to the finish. They were tired of Chief Posey's antics; they wanted him dead.

Posey must have known it. He had been hit in the hip, but he wouldn't go near the town. After a few days, the townspeople and Paiutes saw the smoke curl in the cliffs above Blanding. They knew it must have come from Posey's fire. A sheriff brought in from Salt Lake City freed two of Posey's men to go to Posey with blankets and food and to convince the chief to give himself up. Posey chose to stay where he was.

For days, the people watched the smoke. Some were relieved when the fire went out, others grieved.

Posey's death brought national attention to the Paiute's plight. The federal government stepped in and improved the conditions in San Juan County, increasing the Indians' allotments of food and supplies.

Many called it the last Indian war. Others contended it was never a war at all: it was Posey alone, fighting to the death for a cause already lost.

THE KILLING OF
UTAH'S LAST GRIZZLY BEAR

~ 1923 ~

On warm, moonless summer nights, sheepherders in Utah's mountains wonder what they would do if a cougar, coyote, or black bear got into their herd. Campers and backpackers keep an eye out for animals too. Today, the backcountry is still somewhat wild because environmental laws protect predators in their natural habitats.

In the early part of the twentieth century, such laws didn't exist. No one had heard of environmentalism or endangered species. Ranchers, farmers, and the general citizenry sought to eliminate big predators from the landscape with little thought about the long-term consequences.

That is how, on the night of August 22, 1923, Utah lost one more bit of its wildness when a Malad, Idaho, sheepherder named Frank Clark killed Old Ephraim, the last of the state's great grizzlies.

Clark came to northern Utah's Cache Valley, a place Native Americans called Willow Valley, in 1911 as part-owner of the Ward

Sheep Company. That year, bears reportedly killed 154 adult sheep. In 1912, Clark claimed that he killed thirteen bears, but he could not kill Old Ephraim.

Some say the great Utah grizzly was named after the biblical Ephraim, a patriarchal character the state's Mormons greatly revered. Others say a short story written about a California grizzly called Ephraim gave someone the idea. Whatever the case, Old Ephraim was a magnificent creature. He stood nine feet eleven inches tall, but he moved like a ghost through the thick woods and meadows of Cache Valley, leaving distinctive twelve-inch paw prints. Herders could easily identify Old Ephraim's tracks because he was missing a middle claw on his left hind foot. They seldom, if ever, saw the bear, but they often found his prints near sheep kills.

Frank Clark was a veteran herder who carried his trusty rifle with him nearly all the time. It was a .25-35 caliber carbine, fully loaded with seven steel-ball cartridges. Clark seldom saw his foe, but he studied the grizzly's habits closely, often noticing tracks near the bear's favorite wallows and springs. He would set traps in those places, only to be frustrated when Old Ephraim either removed the trap, unsprung, or tossed the apparatus into the forest. Clark recorded an interesting fact about the grizzly:

> *Old Ephraim was not the greedy killer that some bears seem to be. He would usually kill one sheep, pick it up and carry it into the more remote sections of the mountain and devour it. This is in strict contrast to the actions of some killer bears who may kill as many as 100 sheep in one night. It had become a legend that Old Ephraim never seemed to pick on the same herd twice in succession, but roamed around for several miles in the proxim-*

ity of the spring where he bathed and would only take
one or two sheep from each separate camp.

On August 19, 1923, the sheepherder was hiking near his camp when he found one of the great bear's wallows. Clark tried setting a trap there. The grizzly discovered the trap and, much to the sheepherder's amazement, left it high and dry by digging a small trench to a new wallow. This time, the sheepherder put one trap in the middle of the new wallow and another on the outside edge in case the grizzly found the first trap and backed away from it. This, in Clark's words, is what happened next:

That night was fine and beautiful, a starlight night,
and I was sleeping fine when I was awakened by a
roar and a groan near camp. I had a dog, but not a
sound came from Mr. Dog. I tried to get to sleep, but
no chance, so I got up and put on my shoes but no
trousers. I did take my gun, and walked up the trail. I
did not know it was 'Eph.' In fact, I thought it was a
horse that was down. Eph was in the creek in some
willows and after I had got past him, he let me know
all at once it was not a horse. What should I do? Alone,
the closest human being three miles away, and Eph
between me and camp.

I listened and could hear the chain rattle. So did
my teeth. I decided to get up on the hillside and wait. I
spent many hours up there. I had no way of knowing
how many, listening to Eph's groans and bellows. Day-
light came at last and now it was my turn.

As Clark approached the creek, he saw a small patch of hide and fired at it, grazing the bear. Roaring, Old Ephraim raised up on his hind legs. He had a 14-foot-long chain wound around his right forelimb and a twenty-three-pound bear trap on his front paw.

I saw the most magnificent sight that any man could ever see. I was paralyzed with fear and could not raise my gun. He was coming, still on his hind legs, holding that cussed trap above his head. I was rooted to the earth and let him come within 6 feet of me before I stuck the gun out and pulled the trigger. He fell back, but came again and received five of the remaining six bullets. He had now reached the trail, still on his hind legs. I only had one cartridge left in the gun and that bear would not go down. I went about 20 yards and turned. Eph was coming, still standing up, but my dog, Jennie, was snapping at his heels, so he turned on the dog. I then turned back, and as I got close, he turned again on me, wading along on his hind legs. I could see that he was badly hurt, as at each breath, the blood would spurt from his nostrils, so I gave him the last bullet in the brain. I think I felt sorry I had to do it.

The bear's giant skull, which filled a bushel basket, was sent to the Smithsonian Institution. A group of Boy Scouts erected a crude stone grave at the spot where Clark fired his final shot, near the Lodge Campground in Blacksmith Fork Canyon. Someone added a sign that reads "Here lies Old Ephraim. He gave Frank Clark a good scare." On September 23, 1966, at the same site, the state dedicated a larger monument, which still stands today.

When Frank Clark killed Old Ephraim, no one paid much attention to whether any other grizzly bears still roamed Utah's mountains. Only later did historians realize that Old Ephraim was probably the last.

AB JENKINS IS FAST
ON THE SALT FLATS

~ 1932 ~

DAVID "AB" JENKINS WAS GOING IN CIRCLES, all the while hoping he wasn't losing his mind. Fighting to keep focused, he reminded himself of his job: to become the fastest man alive. If he could concentrate on his driving, he would break the land-speed record for the most miles driven in twenty-four hours.

Jenkins's racetrack was the Bonneville Salt Flats. One of the world's wonders, it is a perfectly flat, dry lake bed made of glistening white salt crystals. In the spring, salt water from the Great Salt Lake covers the flats. By late summer, the water evaporates, leaving a 200-square-mile surface as hard as concrete. The lake bed is so flat and long, you can see the curvature of the earth in it.

At times during his attempt, Jenkins felt as if he was in a haunted house. The roar of his engine deafened him. When night fell, a bright moon behind the mountains cast huge shadows across the salt flats.

Sometimes as he sped by, the shadows turned into giant walls he could almost hear himself crash into.

During the day, the 120-degree heat baked Jenkins. He protected himself from sunburn by covering his face with grease. He had removed the windshield and both fenders from his Pierce-Arrow "12," and the blazing sun seemed to suck every drop of water from his body. The white crystals all around him reflected the sun's rays back into the atmosphere. Shimmering heat waves teased him with mirages. Railroad tracks would appear at one place, then another. Without warning, a locomotive seemed to barrel down the tracks just in front of him, giving him no time to stop.

Jenkins fought against the clock and optical illusions to complete his race. Each time he went around the track, Jenkins looked for landmarks to orient himself. One was the airline beacon on the hill ten miles away. But it kept skipping around. He concentrated on the 4-foot stakes driven into the salt every hundred feet. At night, twenty oil flares lit the track. After each lap, he looked for the large placards his team held up telling him his speed. To keep his mind active, Ab wrote notes while driving over one hundred miles an hour. He threw them to bystanders as he sped past the pit stop.

If he wanted to achieve the record, Ab could not leave his seat, not even during his twelve refueling stops. The tires of his experimental car held together on the hot crusty surface without a single change.

Jenkins's race against time was an experiment, too. He had spent the previous year capturing every automobile hill climbing record in America he attempted. Ab had discussed the great racing potential of Utah's salt flats with the American Automobile Association (AAA), the organization that officiated at these trials. At the time, racers used tracks like those at Daytona Beach, Florida, or Atlantic City, New Jersey. In Ab's opinion, Daytona was too narrow to be safe, and

Atlantic City's circular wooden track would have to be built at a ridiculous 90-degree angle to accommodate higher speeds.

Jenkins wanted to show the world that the Bonneville Salt Flats was the place to set land-speed records. He got his chance when the Pierce-Arrow Automobile Company hired him to help design and test run a new twelve-cylinder car. Together, they managed to increase its horsepower from 130 to 175. Jenkins convinced the company that an attempt at the endurance record would demonstrate the new Pierce-Arrow's high performance. Pierce-Arrow officials scoffed at Ab's claim that he could go 2,400 miles in twenty-four hours, but they gave him the car and six Firestone tires so he could try for the record.

The Utah State Road Commission helped survey and scrape a 10-mile circular track on the salt flats. Friends from Utah, including the Utah State Automobile Club and Chamber of Commerce, helped time Jenkins's run with stopwatches. They thought that was all the AAA rules required for runs of more than 10 miles.

Mirages, heat, and exhaustion could not keep Jenkins from finishing the race. He even surpassed his goal, setting a new record of 2,710 miles in twenty-four hours. Later, the AAA refused to acknowledge his record since they did not officially time the race.

Minutes after finishing his twenty-four-hour run on the salt flats, Jenkins climbed into a plane bound for a Chamber of Commerce luncheon in Salt Lake City. Unfortunately, Jenkins couldn't hear all the praise his admirers piled on him at lunch. The roar of his auto's engine had made him temporarily deaf.

Ab Jenkins returned to the salt flats a year later and set the speed record officially. In the following years, he took turns breaking land-speed records with British drivers Sir Malcolm Campbell, John Cobb, and Captain George Eyston.

In 1950, at the age of sixty-seven, Ab set twenty-six speed records. His top speed was 199 miles per hour. Shortly before his death at age seventy-three, Jenkins finished one trial with an average of 118.375 miles an hour in a stock Pontiac, breaking all existing unlimited and class C stock car records.

Jenkins earned his living as a carpenter and automobile safety engineer; he earned his fame setting land-speed records in his race car, the *Mormon Meteor,* in 1940, 1950, and 1951. For all the automobile racing Ab Jenkins did, though, he maintained that the greatest ride he ever took on the salt flats was on a motorcycle before World War I. Bill Rishel, a motorcycle racing promoter had given him a machine with "vinegar." The machine went so fast that while Ab held onto the handlebars he could stretch his body out flat along the cycle like a boy on a snow sled. He flew along at up to 80 miles an hour in that position. "That was traveling," he said, "and the ride gave my spinal cord more chills than any run I have ever made on the Salt Flats."

Modern racers such as Craig Breedlove in his *Spirit of America* and Art Arfons in his *Green Monster* have continued to race on the salt flats. In the past decade, racers discovered that the salty surface of the flats was disappearing. Working on the lake with the United States Bureau of Land Management and salt industries, the racers are trying to save the salt flats. A new system introduces salt-laden water back onto the flats. Hopefully, the Bonneville Salt Flats will continue to be the place to set land-speed records.

JAPANESE HELD AT
TOPAZ INTERNMENT CAMP

- 1942 -

Seventeen-year-old Kyoku June Omura stopped chatting with her girlfriends as the old relic of a train they were riding jerked to a stop. She looked out the window. Sunlight glared on endless miles of sagebrush. Suddenly, her reality seemed as stark as the surrounding desert.

June had been forced from her comfortable home in East Oakland, California. The United States government sent her to Topaz, a lonely outpost in the desolate western Utah desert, one of several places built to intern 110,000 Japanese Americans.

Anti-Japanese hysteria gripped the United States when Japan bombed Pearl Harbor, Hawaii, on December 7, 1941. All along the West Coast, whites suspected anyone who was Japanese, recent immigrants and American citizens (some second- and third-generation) alike, of being enemy spies. Some simply resented the success the Japanese enjoyed in business and farming. On May 3, 1942, President

Franklin Roosevelt ordered all persons of Japanese ancestry living on the West Coast to leave for internment camps inland within a few days.

When the order came, June's father had to sell everything in his grocery store for pennies. He had not owned his store—Japanese and Chinese Americans were not allowed to own any property—but he did have a substantial bank account. The government would not let him withdraw his money. June's sister had to break her precious Japanese dolls to comply with government instructions. Anything that reflected Japanese culture had to be destroyed—unless friendly neighbors would hide it. Families were forced to give their pets away. The Omuras were told to report to the bus station with only bundles of essential clothing and personal items.

June had spent her whole life in California, and the move to the desert confused and upset her. Her world—a world that revolved around school, dates, music, and movies—suddenly changed. The country she loved suddenly did not trust her.

Looking back, June realized she had lived a double life. She had both a Japanese name, Kyoku, and an American name, June. While her parents, American citizens, wanted June to retain knowledge of and respect for her Japanese roots, they also encouraged her to pursue the American dream. In another month June would have graduated with a degree in dress design from a San Francisco college. Instead, she was being transported to a desolate camp where she would be treated like a prisoner.

The train stopped at Delta, Utah, where June and her family boarded buses for the trip to Topaz. Topaz is in the Great Basin on the dry lake bed of an ancient Pleistocene lake, Lake Bonneville. The living remnant of Lake Bonneville, the Great Salt Lake, lies 140 miles north of Topaz. In the lake bed's alkaline soil, nothing but a few scrawny shrubs survive. Only the mountains to the west break up the flat horizon. The city of barracks surrounded by barbed wire had been hastily slapped together. June knew she and her family would be prisoners here.

The older members of the Japanese community suffered most at Topaz. Successful businessmen were forced to work as cooks and laundry workers. Farmers, accustomed to the fertile valleys of California, eked out small gardens in the alkaline soil. June became an elementary school teacher.

June's paternal grandfather had come to America to help support his family in Japan. He had laughingly boasted that he was the first Japanese cowboy in Lovelock, Nevada. He was accustomed to the desert. Now he shared an 18- by 25-foot room with his son and daughter-in-law and their three daughters, aged nineteen, seventeen, and three. The rooms, simple plywood boxes covered with tar paper, were ovens in the summer when temperatures soared to higher than 100 degrees. In winter, when the mercury fell below the freezing mark, a single potbelly stove gave out the only heat.

The laundry, bathing, and latrine facilities were all communal. More than once, especially during the cold walk to the bathroom, the internees gazed beyond the barbed wire at the guards' quarters. The guards had indoor plumbing. After a while, few remembered what that simple convenience was like.

Like many other internees, June tried to make the best of the situation. She had a full-time job—though she wasn't paid—and an active social life. She saw movies starring Humphrey Bogart and Alan Ladd, but she wasn't allowed to read newspapers. She danced to the music of Glenn Miller, but she couldn't listen to the radio. She didn't need to cook because everyone ate in a common area. At first, the food tasted good. Then June discovered that some casseroles and soups contained tripe and brain. She had never missed traditional Japanese delicacies so much.

Because radios and newspapers were banned in camp, June's family heard nothing at first of the progress of World War II. Then some prisoners' sons, who had served as American soldiers, returned from the battlefield. Soon after the Japanese detention, 113 of the 8,000 internees from camps all over the United States volunteered to serve in the United States armed forces. Though their families were imprisoned, they wanted to prove that they were loyal Americans. Also, they worried that the racism responsible for their internment might not go away after the war. They hoped that heroism on their part would help their families earn a place in society. Every so often, the daily monotony of camp life was broken with news that someone's brother, son, or father had been killed in action. When survivors returned, they told of horrors they wished they had never seen.

The news blackout meant that residents of Topaz were among the last to hear of the bombs dropped on Hiroshima and Nagasaki that ended the war. When they did find out, joy at the American victory was tempered by fears for relatives and friends in Japan, and for their own future. With no homes, money, or jobs, many wondered how they would survive. Internees left the camps a few at a time when they could prove they had a place to go.

The Omuras were among the first families to leave Topaz. June's pregnant sister, married to a Japanese-American soldier, had complications in her pregnancy and was sent to Salt Lake City, where she remained in critical condition. The government allowed June's family to go and take care of her.

June was grateful to leave her barracks. Memories of camp life would remain within her, even though most internees shared little of their internment experience with their children and grandchildren. They faced the task of rebuilding their lives with the same spirit with which they had faced imprisonment. They would work to be accepted as Americans.

PARASKIERS TRAIN FOR WAR AT ALTA

- 1942 -

ON THEIR FIRST RIDE UP THE CHAIR LIFT AT ALTA, the men were nervous. They gazed at the ski run below and considered what they were about to do. The mountain's beauty impressed them. Ten feet of snow covered the craggy slope; here and there, a pine tree poked out at the sky. Most of the 150 paratroopers on the lift had never tried skiing; many had never seen snow.

In wartime, anything is possible. The United States Army decided to train troops to parachute onto a mountain and ski, or paraski. Army leaders envisioned a need to drop soldiers behind enemy lines in mountainous areas for reconnaissance and demolition. The 150 men from Company "B," 503rd Parachute Battalion, were part of an experiment. These soldiers, mostly southerners stationed at Fort Benning, Georgia, would be trained by a group of experts led by Dick Durrance, a ski racer, director of Alta's ski school, and one of the preeminent skiers in the United States at the time.

The chair lift riders looked backwards down the steep slope near the top of Alta, in the Wasatch Mountains east of Salt Lake County.

Perhaps they wondered how a tumble down a mountain compared with a parachute jump—would the landing be any softer?

With this first ride up Collins Gulch, the army intended to acquaint the men with the mountain and provide photographers from the media a photo opportunity. Each soldier was dressed completely in white, from parka to skis. After dismounting the lift, the men showed off their equipment for the press. They had been issued Garand rifles and an assortment of sidearms for close fighting. On their backs, they carried form-fitting rucksacks containing demolition kits. TNT, detonating caps, fuses, drills, and other secret weapons, all in separate insulated rubber containers.

The soldiers took up various combat positions for the photographers; then most of them returned to the lift to ride back down the mountain. The training schedule mandated that ski lessons take place later.

Platoon leader First Lieutenant Bob Carroll decided not to wait until later; he wanted to learn to ski now. Second Lieutenant Ed Thomas, who would follow Bob anywhere, went too, even though he doubted his skiing ability. With patience, perseverance, and instructions from Dick Durrance, the two made it to the bottom, "falling more than skiing," according to Ed. Others in the battalion watched the crazy skiers with interest and amusement. They would get their turn. The men all had previous training in marksmanship, aerial map reading, and the rudiments of meteorology. For six weeks that January and February, for six hours a day, in blizzards and bright snow, the men trained for their ski missions. In small groups, they progressed from snow plows to stem turns and christies. They learned how to cross-country ski in single file so they could pass enemy soldiers undetected.

Working out at high altitude with loaded packs was a new experience that left their limbs weak and their lungs burning. A radio man and medical officer accompanied each group. But the soldiers recognized that, in war, anyone injured in a remote mountain area would have to be considered a casualty.

At Park City, near Alta, the men practiced parachuting onto snow. Jumping in mountain snow is hazardous—high mountain winds, hard, windswept snow, and deep powder can all wreak havoc on a well-planned jump. Luckily, the training began under relatively stable conditions.

On the first pass over the jump site, the plane dropped color-marked cargo bundles containing skis and arms (rifles, machine guns, and mortars). Each group of men knew the color of their bundle.

The C-47 circled over the mountains and back to the jump site. Squatting on benches along the sides of the cabin, the soldiers grinned at each other to hide their nervousness. Every man had carefully packed his own parachute. The commander of the company, Captain Arthur Gorham, sat nearest the door.

At the "stand up" command, the soldiers stood; at "hook up," they snapped their static lines to the anchor cable running down the side of the plane. This automatic rip cord would open the soldiers' chutes as they jumped. On the jump master's "go," the men poured out of the plane, floating and steering themselves toward the bundle marked with their color. When they landed, the men unstrapped the bear paw snowshoes they had carried with them in their jump. With these on their feet, they crossed the deep snow to their bundles without wasted energy.

Another challenging night during the training was spent learning to camp in winter conditions. Ed Thomas dug a hole in the snow and tried to keep warm; it was a long night, nevertheless. Some men simply plopped their sleeping bags on the snow. They soon found that the bag's slick, waterproof covering turned it into a sort of sled. They spent the night trying to keep from sliding downhill. When day dawned and the trucks came to take them back to their barracks near the Salt Lake City airport, the men were relieved.

Most days, a mess crew served the trainees hot food on the slopes. At other times, they had to experiment with dehydrated food. They discovered that at high altitude, steaming stew did not necessarily mean hot stew. Cooking took a lot longer than anyone anticipated.

The training experiment in paraskiing was a difficult physical challenge and a serious preparation for war, but it had its benefits. The scenery was fantastic. Longer treks became cross-country tours, such as the one from Alta over the mountain to Brighton. Many of the men enjoyed their downhill adventures too. Ed Thomas caught the ski bug; it lasted the rest of his life.

The men of the 503rd never did paraski in combat. None of them ever found out why. Some were assigned to units that fought in Europe. Ed Thomas was transferred to a Special Forces type of unit and fought without skis in the mountains of Italy and in southern France. Bob Carroll died fighting at Normandy. Captain Gorham died in Sicily and was posthumously awarded two Distinguished Service Crosses earned in the same twenty-four hour period.

Company B became part of the 503rd Parachute Infantry, which, in an irony of war, fought in the Pacific—including the Corregidor Jump in the Philippines—a long, long way from the snow of Alta.

DICK WILSON BUILDS
THE SLICKROCK BIKE TRAIL

- 1969 -

IT WASN'T UNUSUAL IN THE LATE 1960S to see Dick Wilson riding his motorcycle toward some remote part of southeastern Utah. Wilson was the outdoor editor for the *Moab Times-Independent* and a correspondent for the *Salt Lake Tribune* newspapers. Part of his job involved photographing and writing about new places he explored.

Moab had become a fairly quiet town by then. The uranium mining boom that made it the largest hamlet in southeastern Utah's canyonlands was petering out. In the spring, summer, and fall, tourists used Moab as a base for their explorations: hiking in nearby Arches and Canyonlands national parks, rafting down the Colorado, riding motorcycles or four-wheel-drive vehicles down the old mining roads.

Four miles east of town lay a huge expanse of pale orange rock. Dick Wilson loved riding his knobby-tired dirt bike on it. The two-hundred-million-year-old sandstone, known as slickrock, looked like sand dunes hardened into rolling rock. Cowboys first called it the slickrock because their horses' hooves slipped and slid on the hard, smooth surface. The rock had the opposite effect on Wilson's motorcycle tires. The rubber gripped the surface, making it possible to ride up and down the steep slopes.

In those days, only a few Moab residents knew about the 7,240-acre area of slickrock, sand, and cliffs known as the Sand Flats. Those who did know about it dumped their garbage at a landfill located on the road to the Sand Flats. Wilson dubbed it "the world's most scenic dump." Anywhere else, the dump site would have merited protection as a national park or monument, or at least a state park. But fantastic scenery is common around Moab, and most residents drove right past the dump and the Sand Flats on their way to the cool forests of the La Sal Mountains.

Decades later, Wilson explained why he brought the Sand Flats area into the public eye. "I had a dream that I would some day see that dump as an attractive campground. I had to watch columns of black smoke rising out of the dump. The place was as beautiful as any national park in the nation, and it wasn't being appreciated. There must have been another place to put a city dump."

Hollywood producers knew the Sand Flats area well. Once, covered wagons filled with actors had traveled up the dusty trail using the scenic setting as a symbol of the Old West. Wilson began putting together a new kind of trail. Rubbing his black tire treads on the rock every hundred yards or so, he crudely marked out two loop trails on the slickrock. He took friends and relatives along the trails to some of his favorite places, hidden among the smooth rolling hills of rock. Off-highway motorcycles—dirt bikes—could use Wilson's markings to take off-road trips.

Wilson began naming some of the features along the trail. On one ride, he stopped to gaze over the edge of a cliff at a beautiful natural arch. As he took a handkerchief out of his pocket, a gust of wind grabbed it. Wilson watched the hanky drift down through the middle of the arch and out of sight. Then it blew right back up and into his hand again. He called the rock formation Updraft Arch, a moniker that stuck.

Another time, Wilson looked down into Negro Bill Canyon and saw a beautiful natural bridge spanning a clear blue pool of water. The pool reminded Wilson of Morning Glory Pool in Yellowstone National Park. He dubbed the bridge Morning Glory Bridge.

Wilson gave one of the most prominent rock formations on the trail the name Shrimp Rock, in honor of a unique desert life form: an unusual type of shrimp. Wilson heard that the creature spends its short life span breeding and laying eggs in the small potholes along the trails—only when the holes are full of rainwater. The eggs then lie dormant, sometimes for years, until a rainstorm fills the puddles with water again, and the cycle repeats.

One of Wilson's favorite places to ride was a rock pockmarked with soft spots that had collapsed into funnel-shaped pits. He named it Swiss Cheese Ridge.

The Bureau of Land Management (BLM) owned much of the Sand Flats area above Moab. Wilson decided to ask the BLM if he could construct a motorcycle trail there. BLM employee Doug Wood helped Wilson put together a plan for a formally designated recreational trail for lightweight motorcycles built to be ridden off-road.

The plan encountered little opposition. Mining trails crisscrossed the area and cattle had overgrazed it. Moab residents believed the area had little or no value; ranchers had no use for it. Such a trail might even help the economy by bringing a few more tourists to Moab.

When Wilson's idea gained formal approval, he replaced the tread markings, using paint to mark the rock every fifty feet or so. Years later, Wilson described his experience working with the BLM to complete the trail. "This was the greatest example of cooperation between government and citizens that I have ever seen. I was a small-town citizen who suggested an idea to the BLM. I marked the trail for them. They brought in a paint crew and finished it up. Without that kind of cooperation, it would not have happened."

On July 22, 1969, Wilson's trail was formally dedicated. F. C. Koziol, then director of the Utah Division of Parks and Recreation, spoke at the ceremony. "This is one way the BLM is meeting the recreation explosion crisis," Koziol told a small group of about twenty motorcyclists who gathered for the dedication. "It closely parallels the first landing on the moon, being opened during the same week, and requiring a certain amount of pioneering on the part of those who originated the idea."

No one who attended the trail dedication imagined what the Slickrock Bike Trail would be like twenty-five years later. The off-road, human-powered vehicle called the mountain bike had not yet been invented. In the 1980s and 1990s, knobby-tired mountain bikes became popular with outdoor enthusiasts. The slickrock trail, originally built for motorcycles, became the world's most famous mountain-biking route.

By 1996, close to 160,000 mountain bikers a year were traveling to Moab. They came from all over the world to ride the 1.7-mile-long practice loop and the 9.6-mile-long main loop that Dick Wilson marked in 1969. Dozens of outdoor magazine covers featured the Slickrock Bike Trail. A tourist boom turned the once sleepy ex-mining town of Moab into the mountain biking capital of the world.

Wilson left Moab in 1972 for a computer job in southern California. He gave up motorcycles for mountain bikes, but by 1997, he still hadn't returned to ride the trail he built. He did keep track of the trail through the grapevine, however, and he offered this challenge to the hundreds of thousands of bikers who use it each year. "If the crowds are causing a terrible impact on the juniper trees, cactus, and pinyon pines in the area, they have missed the whole point of the trail. This is the most indestructible trail in the world. The game the bikers should play is to try and stay on the rock and see how far they can go without riding on the sand and fragile environment. And campers should bring their own firewood."

Wilson's Slickrock Bicycle Trail has the capacity to provide thrills and inspiration far into the future. If mountain bikers heed his advice, it will.

THE 2002 WINTER OLYMPICS

- 2002 -

UTAH'S QUEST TO HOST THE WINTER OLYMPICS proved long and often quixotic. It took almost a generation of bidding—rife with rejections—before the International Olympic Committee selected Salt Lake City to host the 2002 Winter Games.

Government leaders debated ways to finance the Games, environmentalists worried about protecting Utah's canyons and watersheds, and opponents warned of taxpayer debt. Add to that a bribery scandal that shook up the organizational structure of the Salt Lake Organizing Committee after it was revealed that some International Olympic Committee members were given special treatment. And, finally, there were the attacks of September 11, 2001, on New York City and Washington, D.C., that put the world on edge and added tremendously to the cost of providing security.

But, when what the *Salt Lake Tribune* would call "seventeen remarkable days" ended on Febuary 24, 2002, with a closing ceremony that featured dinosaurs and joyous athletes, even skeptics came away impressed.

Salt Lake City might have been the official host city of the XIX Winter Games, but it was a historic effort for *all* parts of Utah, with new facilities springing up from Provo to Logan across the Wasatch Front to host the Games.

The entire state seemed to show up for the Olympic torch run which began on a frosty morning at the Delicate Arch—an iconic natural feature that to many symbolizes Utah—and wound its way through towns and neighborhoods large and small.

That torch run culminated on February 8 at a newly remodeled Rice-Eccles Stadium on the University of Utah Campus, where, in front of a crowd that included dignitaries and leaders from around the world, the 1980 U.S. "Miracle on Ice" hockey team—led by Captain Mike Eruzione—lit a modernistic torch on the south end of the football stadium. It was time for the Games to begin. Athletes from seventy-seven nations marched into the stadium on a night that seemed to bring a troubled world together, if only for a moment.

The opening ceremony, on a football stadium field that became a giant ice-skating rink, celebrated Utah's diversity—showcasing Mormon pioneers and American Indians, some of the world's top entertainers, and fireworks built around a theme of "Light the Fire Within." It was a magic night, an evening experienced by a worldwide television audience. Folks in the packed stadium filled with folks who will never forget the extravaganza, tinged with the emotion of a post-9/11 world and fueled by a state that had struggled since the 1960s to show itself was capable of hosting such a show.

"Walking into Rice-Eccles Stadium with all those people chanting 'USA,' I think my pulse went out the top of the stadium and over the Wasatch Mountains," commented Ann Swisshelm, a U.S. curler.

"I thought I was floating 2 feet off the ground," said U.S. cross country skier Kikkan Randall. "It was everything it was supposed to be and more."

For the next seventeen days, Utah went about proving to the world it was more than up to the task of hosting the Games. Transportation to events in Ogden, Park City, the Heber Valley, and West Valley City went more smoothly than expected. Thousands of fans cheered athletes who skied, snowboarded, ice skated, curled, luged, and bobsledded at state-of-the-art facilities.

At night, at a specially designed medals plaza and stadium in a Salt Lake City parking lot, thousands would gather not only to see the gold, silver, and bronze medals awarded but to enjoy featured bands, too—from Brooks and Dunn to the Barenaked Ladies to Smashmouth.

The streets of the city filled like never before as the Olympics became not only an athletic competition but a true cultural event with rock bands, modern dance, jazz music, and even an Army band concert. Ticket scalpers gathered on street corners, bargaining and haggling over prices to all the big events such as the opening and closing ceremonies, the women's figure skating final, and the hockey gold medal game. Many just came to watch the fun and wander the streets, doing some Olympic pin trading, trying to buy a "Roots" beret that the U.S. athletes wore as part of their uniform, or just basking in what became the largest party Utah would ever see.

On one memorable night, as the world watched American Sarah Hughes win a gold medal in the women's figure skating event, many gathered to sit on straw bales next to a giant television screen at Washington Square, home of Salt Lake City's gothic-looking City-County Building. They could have easily watched the event in front of their home televisions like the rest of the world. But the Olympics are about connecting people from all walks of life, and it seemed somehow fitting to share the experience.

The events produced many other memorable moments— Picabo Street's last Olympic Ski, the speedskating excitement of American Apolo Anton Ohno, the Canadian hockey team reclaiming gold, the emergence of Bode Miller as a U.S. skiing star, Chris Witty winning the 1000-meter skating gold, snowboarder Kelly Clark earning gold, and the joy of veteran U.S. bobsledder Brian Shimer winning his first Olympic medal in his fourth Games.

The controversy of the 2002 Olympics was the judging of the pairs ice skating; many thought Canadians Jamie Sale and David Pelletier were robbed of a gold medal given to Russians Elena Berezhnaya and Anton Sikharulidze. A French judge was accused of bowing to pressure to give the Russians the medal, and the International Olympic Committee eventually awarded *both* pairs gold medals.

Yet, by the time the closing ceremony featured dinosaurs named Donny and Marie after Utah's famous Osmonds, nearly everyone involved was calling Salt Lake City's Olympics a huge success. Much to the surprise of skeptics, the Games turned a profit, paying off taxpayers' investments in infrastructure and leaving a legacy to maintain the facilities for future generations. The Olympics also helped revive the political career of Mitt Romney, who rescued a Utah effort reeling from revelations of the bribery scandal.

Perhaps most important, the Games left a legacy of facilities, including a speed skating rink, bobsled and luge track, ski jumping hill, and biathlon and nordic skiing tracks, that will serve athletes for generations. Salt Lake City's 2002 Winter Olympics will provide the facilities to help future Olympians realize their dreams of gold and perhaps develop native Utahns into world-class athletes.

UTAH FACTS & TRIVIA

Utah is named for the local Ute Indians. Ute means "high place." The original settlers wanted to name the territory Deseret, but because of the name's religious significance to Mormons, the federal government insisted on Utah.

The state symbol is a beehive, which stands for industry. It also connotes the pioneer value of the community working together.

The state tree is the Colorado blue spruce.

The state animal is the Rocky Mountain elk.

The state bird is the California Gull. According to folklore, this bird averted a famine in pioneer times by devouring crickets that were attacking the pioneers' crops.

The state fish was recently changed from Rainbow Trout, an imported fish, to the Bonneville Cutthroat Trout, a fish native to Utah.

The state flower is the sego lily. The bulb of this flower is edible. Native Americans showed the pioneers how to subsist on the bulb during times of famine. They also showed the settlers how to mash roasted crickets and bake them into bread.

The state fossil is the Allosaurus, of which Utah has many. Utah is also home to T-rex and Utahraptor fossils.

The state gem is topaz.

The state mineral is copper while its official state rock is coal.

The cherry is the official state fruit.

Indian ricegrass is Utah's official grass.

The sugar beet and onion double as the state's official vegetables.

The Dutch Oven is Utah's official cooking pot.

The square dance is the state's official dance.

Utah's state tourism "brand" is "Life Elevated."

Industry is the state motto.

Utah has both a state star, the Duhbe, and a state astronomical symbol, the Beehive Cluster.

Utah has five national parks, forty-five state parks, seven national monuments, one national historic area, two national recreation areas, and hundreds of thousands of acres of national forests and Bureau of Land Management lands. In fact, over half the state is public land.

Utah's Escalante-Grand Staircase National Monument was dedicated in 1997, making it one of the nation's newest monuments.

Water in the Great Salt Lake has been measured at about 25 percent salt.

While no fish live in the Great Salt Lake, it is home to brine shrimp. Brine shrimping is a multimillion dollar industry in Utah. The shorebird populations that stop to feed on brine shrimp at the lake during their migrations give the lake hemispheric significance.

Utah is famous for its powder skiing. Powder snow has a lower moisture content than regular snow.

Eleven ski resorts are located within an hour's drive of the Salt Lake International Airport.

As of 2006, the state's population was 2.5 million and growing. The majority, 76 percent, live along the Wasatch Front between Ogden and Provo. Salt Lake County has 950,000 residents.

Most of the 5 percent of Utah's land that is arable also lies along the Wasatch Front. The rest of the state is basically bedrock, a geologist's paradise.

Utah's annual precipitation is between 8 and 10 inches. Most precipitation falls in the form of winter snow.

Utah is the eleventh largest state.

The state's highest point is King's Peak at 13,528 feet.

The state's lowest point is Beaver Dam Wash at 2,000 feet above sea level. The Mohave Desert, the Great Basin, and the Colorado Plateau converge in the Wash, creating a unique area. This unusual habitat contains the topography, plants, and animals of all three regions.

Eighty percent of the tourists who visit Utah come by car; 20 percent come by air.

In 1996 tourism brought $3.8 billion to Utah's economy.

Forty-nine percent of Utah's tourists come for outdoor/adventure activities.

Temple Square in Salt Lake City receives the most tourists with more than five million visitors a year.

Sixty-two-point-four percent of Utahns are on the Mormon Church membership rolls as of 2006.

Although it is against the state law and Mormon Church teaching, approximately 20,000 excommunicated Mormons discreetly practice polygamy.

Utahns consume four times as much Jell-O as the residents of any other state. This has something to do with church potluck dinners. Lime is the favorite flavor.

Utah has the highest birthrate in the United States.

Kennecott Copper Mine to the west of Salt Lake City is North America's largest and oldest open-pit copper mine. It produces copper, gold, silver, and molybdenum.

Peters Sink, between Logan and Garden City, is nationally known for its record-setting cold temperatures. The spot's lowest recorded temperature was -69 degrees Fahrenheit on February 1, 1985. Coincidentally, Utah's hottest temperature was recorded in 1985 too: the mercury at St. George, in the south, hit 117 degrees Fahrenheit on July 5.

Paul Bunyon's Potty, Molly's Nipple, Horsethief Bottom, and Sweet Alice Canyon are not X-rated movies, just some of the names chosen to describe the fantastic geologic formations in the national parks of the Colorado Plateau.

Philo Farnsworth, inventor of the television, was born in a log cabin in Indian Creek, Utah, in 1906.

Jake Garn, then a Utah senator, orbited the earth in the *Discovery* shuttle in April 1985.

Actor Robert Redford owns Sundance Ski Resort and organizes the Sundance Film Institute, both in Utah.

SUGGESTED FURTHER READING

Alexander, Thomas G. *Utah: The Right Place.* Salt Lake City: Gibbs Smith, Publisher, 1995.

Anderson, Nels. *Desert Saints: The Mormon Frontier in Utah.* Chicago: University of Chicago Press, 1942.

Arrington, Leonard J. *Brigham Young: American Moses.* New York: Alfred A. Knopf, 1985.

Backus, Anna Jean. *Mountain Meadows Witness: The Life and Times of Bishop Philip Klingensmith.* Spokane, Wash.: The Arthur H. Clark Company, 1996.

Bashore, Melvin, and Scott Crump. *Riverton: The Story of a Utah Country Town.* Riverton, Utah: Riverton Historical Society, 1994.

Berry, Don. *A Majority of Scoundrels.* New York: Harper Brothers, 1961.

Brooks, George R., ed. *Jedediah S. Smith: His Personal Account of the Journey to California 1826–27.* Glendale, Calif.: The Arthur H. Clark Company, 1977.

Brooks, Juanita. *John D. Lee.* Glendale, Calif.: The Arthur H. Clark Company, 1962.

Carr, Stephen. "Knightsville." In *The Historical Guide to Utah Ghost Towns.* Salt Lake City: Western Epics, 1986.

Carter, Kate. *Riders of the Pony Express.* Salt Lake City: Daughters of the Utah Pioneers, 1952.

———.*Utah and the Pony Express.* Salt Lake City: Daughters of the Utah Pioneers, 1988.

Dilley, J.W. *History of the Scofield Mine Disaster.* Provo, Utah: The Skelton Publishing Co., 1900.

Foner, Philip S. *The Case of Joe Hill.* New York: International Publishers, 1965.

Harris, Beth Kay. "Jesse Knight." In *The Towns of Tintic.* Denver: Sage Books, 1961.

Jenkins, Ab, and Wendell Ashton. *The Salt of the Earth.* Los Angeles: Clymer Motors, 1945.

Jessee, Dean C., ed. *My Dear Son: Letters of Brigham Young to His Sons.* Salt Lake City: Deseret Book Company, 1974.

Kelly, Charles. *The Outlaw Trail: The Story of Butch Cassidy and the "Wild Bunch."* New York: Bonanza Books, 1959.

Kelner, Alexis. *Skiing in Utah: A History.* Salt Lake City, 1980.

McCune, Alice Paxman. "Knightsville." In *History of Juab County.* Springville, Utah: Juab County Daughters of Utah Pioneers, 1947.

Miller, David Eugene. *Hole-in-the-Rock: An Epic in the Colonization of the Great American West.* Salt Lake City: University of Utah Press, 1959.

Morgan, Dale. *The Great Salt Lake.* Salt Lake City: University of Utah Press, 1995.

———. *Jedediah Smith and the Opening of the West.* Lincoln: University of Nebraska Press, 1953.

Mulder, William, and Russell A. Mortensen, eds. *Among the Mormons: Historic Accounts by Contemporary Observers.* Lincoln: University of Nebraska Press, 1958.

Pointer, Larry. *In Search of Butch Cassidy.* Norman: University of Oklahoma Press, 1977.

Powell, J.W. *Canyons of the Colorado.* New York: Flood and Vincent, 1895. Reprinted as *The Exploration of the Colorado River and Its Canyons.* New York: Dover Publications, Inc., 1961.

Robinson, Adonis Findlay. *History of Kane County.* Salt Lake City: Daughters of Utah Pioneers Kane County Camp, 1970.

Settle, Raymond and Mary. *Saddles and Spurs.* Lincoln: University of Nebraska Press, 1955.

Smith, Gibbs. *Joe Hill.* Salt Lake City: Gibbs Smith, Inc./Peregrine Smith Books, 1984.

Stavis, Barrie. *The Man Who Never Died.* New York: Haven Press, 1954.

Utley, Robert M. *A Life Wild and Perilous: Mountain Men and the Paths to the Pacific.* New York: Henry Holt and Company, 1997.

Watt, Ronald G. *A History of Carbon County.* Salt Lake City: Utah State Historical Society, 1997.

White, Jean Bickmore. "Martha H. Cannon." In *Sister Saints: Women in Early Utah.* Edited by Vicky Burgess-Olson. Provo, Utah: Brigham Young University, 1978.

INDEX

ABOUT THE AUTHORS

The late Gayen Wharton was a native Utahn who was active in environmental education. As an elementary school teacher, she was a national "Project Learning Tree Educator of the Year." She died of ovarian cancer in 2004.

Tom Wharton has worked at the *Salt Lake Tribune* since 1970 and has served as outdoor editor since 1978. He was the president of the Outdoor Writers Association of America from 1998 to 1999. He served twenty-one years in the Utah National Guard.

The Whartons, both graduates of the University of Utah, have four children. This is the fourth book they co-wrote.